IPMA Project Excellence Baseline

Owner and author of this document:

Legal Address:
International Project Management Association (IPMA)
c/o Advokaturbüro Maurer & Stäger, Fraumünsterstrasse 17
Postfach 2018, CH-8022 Zurich, Switzerland

Operational Address:
International Project Management Association (IPMA),
P.O. Box 1167 NL-3860 BD Nijkerk, The Netherlands

Copyright:
©2016 International Project Management Association (IPMA®)
All rights reserved (including those of translation into other languages).
No part of this document may be reproduced in any form – by photo print,
microfilm, or any other means – nor transmitted or translated into
a machine language without written permission.

IPMA, IPMA ICB, IPMA Level A, IPMA Level B, IPMA Level C, IPMA Level D
and IPMA Delta are registered trademarks protected by law in most countries.
IPMA: IPMA Project Excellence Baseline® (IPMA PEB). Version 1.0.1

ISBN Paperback: 9789401811941
ISBN eBook: 9789401811958
ISBN ePub: 9789401811965
Publisher: Van Haren Publishing, 's-Hertogenbosch – The Netherlands

Editorial team (in alphabetical order):
Michael Boxheimer (Germany)
Dr. Sonja Ellmann (Germany)
Mary Koutintcheva (Switzerland)
Erik Mansson (Germany) – project manager
Alexey Polkovnikov (Russia)
Pau Lian Staal-Ong (The Netherlands)
Grzegorz Szałajko (Poland) – the leading editor

Sub-editor:
Ros James (The United Kingdom)

Graphical Design:
Maša Poljanec (Croatia)
Dana Kowal (Poland) - diagrams and redesign for version 1.0.1

Proofreading:
Deborah Boyce (The United Kingdom)

Foreword

Our society is rapidly moving away from routine tasks and permanent organisations towards more fluid structures where the project form is the most natural way of organising most activities. At the same time, society is having to cope with unprecedented complexity due to factors such as climate change, rapidly changing markets, poverty and financial crisis. Alongside these, there are additional factors such as the trend among stakeholders to promote their interests actively and the way that objectives increasingly tend to change during the lifecycle of projects. For all these reasons, it is important to understand the building blocks of project excellence.

This standard, the IPMA Project Excellence Baseline® (IPMA PEB), is designed to promote excellence in managing projects and programmes, and complements our previous standards for individual competences IPMA Individual Competence Baseline (IPMA ICB®) and organisational competences in managing projects IPMA Organisational Competence Baseline (IPMA OCB®). The main target audiences for the IPMA PEB are senior managers, project, programme and portfolio managers (including Project Management Office (PMO) and project staff) as well as project excellence assessors, consultants, trainers and coaches.

The IPMA PEB is based on many years of practical experience in assessing project excellence for the annual IPMA Global Project Excellence Award. Such assessments have been carried out using the IPMA Project Excellence Model (IPMA PEM), which has enabled the assessment of projects from all kinds of industries and geographical locations.

As part of the project to publish a new IPMA standard for project excellence, we have reviewed and enhanced the IPMA PEM to ensure it takes account of recent developments in project management. In this regard, I am particularly pleased to announce that we now expect every excellent project to consider sustainability and the environment with a long-term perspective, not as an option but rather as the default. In other words, we have moved away from the past practice of allowing each project to decide what is in scope and what is not, to one that makes it clear that consideration of sustainability and impact on the environment are prerequisites for project excellence.

We would like to thank the project team (Ewa Bednarczyk, Michael Boxheimer, Dr. Sonja Ellmann, Mary Koutintcheva, Erik Mansson, Alexey Polkovnikov, Pau Lian Staal-Ong and Grzegorz Szalajko), our energy project experts (Nassereddin Eftekhar, Professor Paul Gardiner, Ivano Ianelli and Gholamreza Safakish) as well as our sounding board (Philippe Brun, Marco Buijnsters, Peter Coesmans, Brian Cracknell, Professor Ronggui Ding, Cedrik Lanz, Mary McKinlay, Frank Menter, Dr. Steve Milner and Peter Milsom) for all their efforts and contributions.

We would also like to thank all the national and international IPMA Global Project Excellence Award assessors and judges for their valuable input in improving the awards process and the IPMA Project Excellence Model.

IPMA PEB is another milestone that will help us move the project management profession forward!

Reinhard Wagner
IPMA President

Executive summary

IPMA offers a wide range of beneficial services for individuals, projects and organisations, starting with the Four-Level Certification (4-L-C) in project management for individuals and the Two-Level Certification for PM consultants. In addition, IPMA offers the IPMA Delta® as a service for organisations interested in improving their performance in project management. IPMA Delta is a service to assess and certify organisations in a broad and thorough way. It is offered by independent Certification Bodies (CB) of IPMA Member Associations (MA). Three standards are used during the IPMA Delta assessment – the IPMA Individual Competence Baseline (IPMA ICB®) to assess selected individuals; the IPMA Project Excellence Baseline® (IPMA PEB) and the IPMA Project Excellence Model (IPMA PEM), to assess selected projects and/or programmes; and the IPMA Organisational Competence Baseline (IPMA OCB®) to assess the organisation as a whole. Thus, with the publication of the IPMA PEB 1.0.1, IPMA has now put in place the third and final baseline.

The main purpose of the IPMA PEB is to describe the concept of excellence in managing projects and programmes. It also serves as a guide to organisations in assessing the ability of their projects and programmes to achieve project excellence. As the baseline is derived from Total Quality Management (TQM) and related models (e.g. EFQM), organisations that have already dealt with these concepts will have no problem in applying and using the IPMA PEB. The baseline is designed to be of use in any context and regardless of the specific industry, sector or project management approach.

The IPMA PEB focuses on a project or programme, complementing two other IPMA standards:
- IPMA ICB – designed to assess individual competences of project/programme/portfolio leaders;
- IPMA OCB – designed to assess competences of organisations that run projects.

The six most typical user groups of the IPMA PEB are:
- Senior management;
- Project, programme and portfolio managers, heads/managers of PMOs and PfMOs;
- Knowledge, quality and process managers;
- Researchers and educators (teachers, trainers);
- Project Excellence Award trainers and assessors;
- Consultants.

The IPMA Project Excellence Model (IPMA PEM) is a core element of the IPMA PEB and is designed to provide guidelines for assessing a project or programme.

It is an adaptable and open assessment method designed for various purposes:
- Driving continuous improvement in projects;
- Regular monitoring of a project's ability to deliver sustainable results on different levels (objectives, customer, employee, stakeholder, environment);
- Assessment and continuous improvement of project management methods;
- Recognition of projects that prove to be excellent based on the IPMA PEM assessment;
- Recognition of projects that are striving for excellence;
- Recognition of excellent leadership and management performance;
- Complementing project audit tools;
- Complementing project management maturity assessment tools.

The three key areas of the model are:

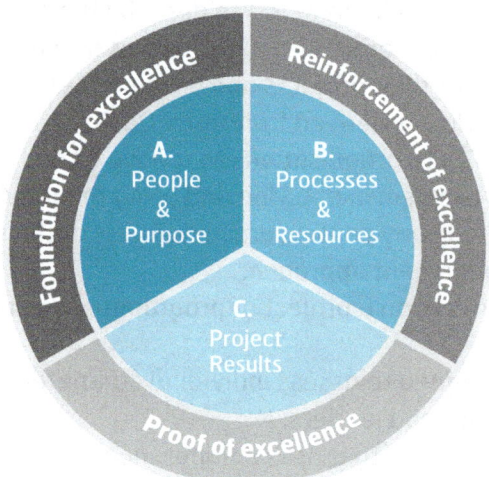

- **People & Purpose** – This area is considered to be the foundation of project excellence. The right people, led and supported by excellent leaders, all sharing a common vision for success, are crucial to drive improvements in a project and help the project achieve more than the established standards.
- **Processes & Resources** – This area represents practices necessary to reinforce excellence through sound processes and adequate resources, used in an efficient and sustainable way. It also serves as a basis for securing the outcome of innovation, turning it into a solid starting point for further waves of improvements.

- **Project Results** – The project management approach can only be excellent if it leads to outstanding, sustainable results for all key stakeholders. This area complements the first two with necessary proof of excellent results as defined by the project stakeholders.

These areas are inspired by and closely related to the EFQM criteria often used for the assessment of organisational excellence. This deliberate link helps organisations that use EFQM to extend their excellence efforts into projects while keeping consistency with their organisation-wide initiatives.

The following project values can be secured by ensuring close interaction between the main areas of the model:
- **Performance;**
- **Effectiveness and efficiency;**
- **Reliability;**
- **Flexibility;**
- **Continuous improvement;**
- **Scalability;**
- **Sustainability.**

Table of Contents

Foreword   5

Executive summary   7

Table of Contents   11

List of figures   14

List of tables   15

Abbreviations and acronyms   16

Terms and definitions   17

1. Introduction   **21**

1.1. IPMA PEB links to IPMA OCB and IPMA ICB   24

2. Purposes and intended users   **27**

2.1. Purpose of the IPMA Project Excellence Baseline   27

2.2. Typical user groups of the IPMA PEB   28

3. The project in its context   **33**

3.1. What is a project?   33

    3.1.1. The project in an organisation   33

    3.1.2. The project as a temporary organisation   34

    3.1.3. Processes in a project   35

3.2. A project in its external context   36

3.3. A project in its organisational context   38

    3.3.1. Organisational context   38

    3.3.2. Project governance   38

    3.3.3. The project in the context of a programme and portfolio   39

Table of Contents

4. Introducing project excellence — 43

4.1. The concept of excellence — 43

4.2. The concept of project excellence — 44

4.3. Continuous improvement as a foundation for excellence — 45

4.4. The role of sustainability — 47

4.5. The role of leadership — 50

4.6. The link between competence and excellence — 51

5. Introduction to the Project Excellence Model — 55

5.1. Principles behind the model design — 55

5.2. Structure of the model — 56

5.3. Areas of the model and interpretation of the overall results — 57

5.4. Interactions between the areas of the model — 60

5.5. Business value delivery using IPMA PEM — 61

5.6. The model criteria — 62

6. Assessment of project excellence — 71

6.1. Purposes and approaches to the project excellence assessment — 71

6.2. Assessment of project excellence in a project lifecycle — 75

6.3. Scope of the assessment in projects, programmes and portfolios — 77

6.4. The role and competences of project excellence assessors — 82

6.5. The assessment process — 84

6.6. Scoring approach — 86

Table of Contents

Annex A: Description of the Project Excellence Model	**91**
A. People & Purpose	92
B. Processes & Resources	102
C. Project Results	107
Annex B: Scoring tables for the IPMA Project Excellence Model	**117**
Scoring table for People & Purpose and Processes & Resources areas	118
Scoring table for Customer, Project Team and Other Stakeholder Satisfaction criteria	119
Scoring table for Project Results criteria	120
Annex C: The IPMA Global Project Excellence Award assessment and its benefits	**121**
The IPMA Global Project Excellence Award assessment	122
The IPMA Global Project Excellence Award benefits	125
References	**127**

List of figures

Figure	Title	Page
Figure 1-1	IPMA PEB as a driver for project management approach, control framework and/or control model	21
Figure 3-1	External versus internal project context	36
Figure 4-1	The use of the PDCA cycle of continuous improvement	45
Figure 5-1	Interpretation of the model areas	57
Figure 5-2	Mapping between IPMA PEM areas and EFQM criteria	58
Figure 5-3	Leadership-driven project	58
Figure 5-4	Process-driven project	59
Figure 5-5	Balanced project	59
Figure 5-6	Interaction between the model areas	60
Figure 5-7	Value delivered through interaction between model areas	61
Figure 5-8	The IPMA PEM criteria	62
Figure 6-1	The use of IPMA PEM at various stages of the project lifecycle	75
Figure 6-2	Scope of the overall programme management assessment	79
Figure 6-3	Scope of the individual project assessment within a programme	80
Figure 6-4	Scope of assessment of an entire programme	80
Figure 6-5	Criteria for scoring areas A and B	86
Figure 6-6	Criteria for scoring stakeholder satisfaction	87
Figure 6-7	Criteria for scoring project results	89

List of tables

Tables	Title	Page
Table 1	Abbreviations and acronyms	16
Table 2	Terms and definitions	17
Table 3	Scoring table for People & Purpose and Processes & Resources areas	118
Table 4	Scoring table for Customer, Project Team and Other Stakeholder Satisfaction criteria	119
Table 5	Scoring table for Project Results criteria	120

Abbreviations and acronyms

Abbreviation or acronym	Explanation
4-L-C	IPMA Universal Four-Level-Certification
CB	Certification Body
EFQM	European Foundation for Quality Management
GPM	German Project Management Association
HR	Human resources
AMBo	IPMA Award Management Board
IPMA ICB	IPMA Individual Competence Baseline
IPMA	International Project Management Association
ISO	International Organization for Standardization
KPI	Key performance indicator
MA	Member Association of IPMA
IPMA OCB	IPMA Organisational Competence Baseline
PDCA	Plan-Do-Check-Act (Deming Cycle)
IPMA PEB	IPMA Project Excellence Baseline
IPMA PEM	IPMA Project Excellence Model
PMO	Project management office
PfMO	Portfolio management office
ROI	Return On Investment
TLA	Team Lead Assessor
TQM	Total Quality Management

Table 1: Abbreviations and acronyms

Terms and definitions

Term	Definition
Assessment	Mechanism to evaluate competences by one or more means, such as self-assessments or third party assessments.
Certification	A set of activities following the certification scheme within the framework of the certification processes and system.
Competence	Demonstrated ability to apply knowledge and skills. [ISO 9000]
Continuous improvement	Recurring activity to increase the ability to fulfil requirements. [ISO 9000]
Culture	Set of shared views, values, or beliefs guiding people consciously or unconsciously through their actions.
Effectiveness	Extent to which planned activities are realised and planned results achieved. [ISO 9000]
Efficiency	Relationship between the result achieved and the resources used. [ISO 9000]
Excellence	Demonstrated performance which is exceptionally good and which exceeds ordinary contemporary standards.
Governance	The system by which organisations are directed and controlled. [ISO 38500]
Management	Coordinated activities to direct and control an organisation. [ISO 9000]
Management system	System to establish policy and objectives in order to achieve those objectives. [ISO 9000]
Organisation	Group of people and facilities with an arrangement of responsibilities, authorities and relationships. [ISO 9000]
Process	Set of interrelated or interacting activities, which transforms inputs into outputs. [ISO 9000]

Project leader	A person who has a role or position in a permanent or project organisation that makes him/her accountable for defining and/or enabling success of the business case, the project or its part (e.g. project sponsor, project manager, team leader).
Stakeholder	Any individual, group or organisation who may affect, be affected by, or perceive themselves to be affected by, a decision or activity. [ISO 38500]
Strategy	An organisation's overall plan of development, describing the effective use of resources in support of the organisation in its future activities. [ISO 38500]
Sustainable development	Development that meets the needs of the present without compromising the ability of future generations to meet their own needs. [ISO 26000]
System	Set of interrelated or interacting elements. [ISO 9000]
Top management	Person or group of people directing and controlling an organisation at the highest level. [ISO 9000]

Table 2: Terms and definitions

1. Introduction

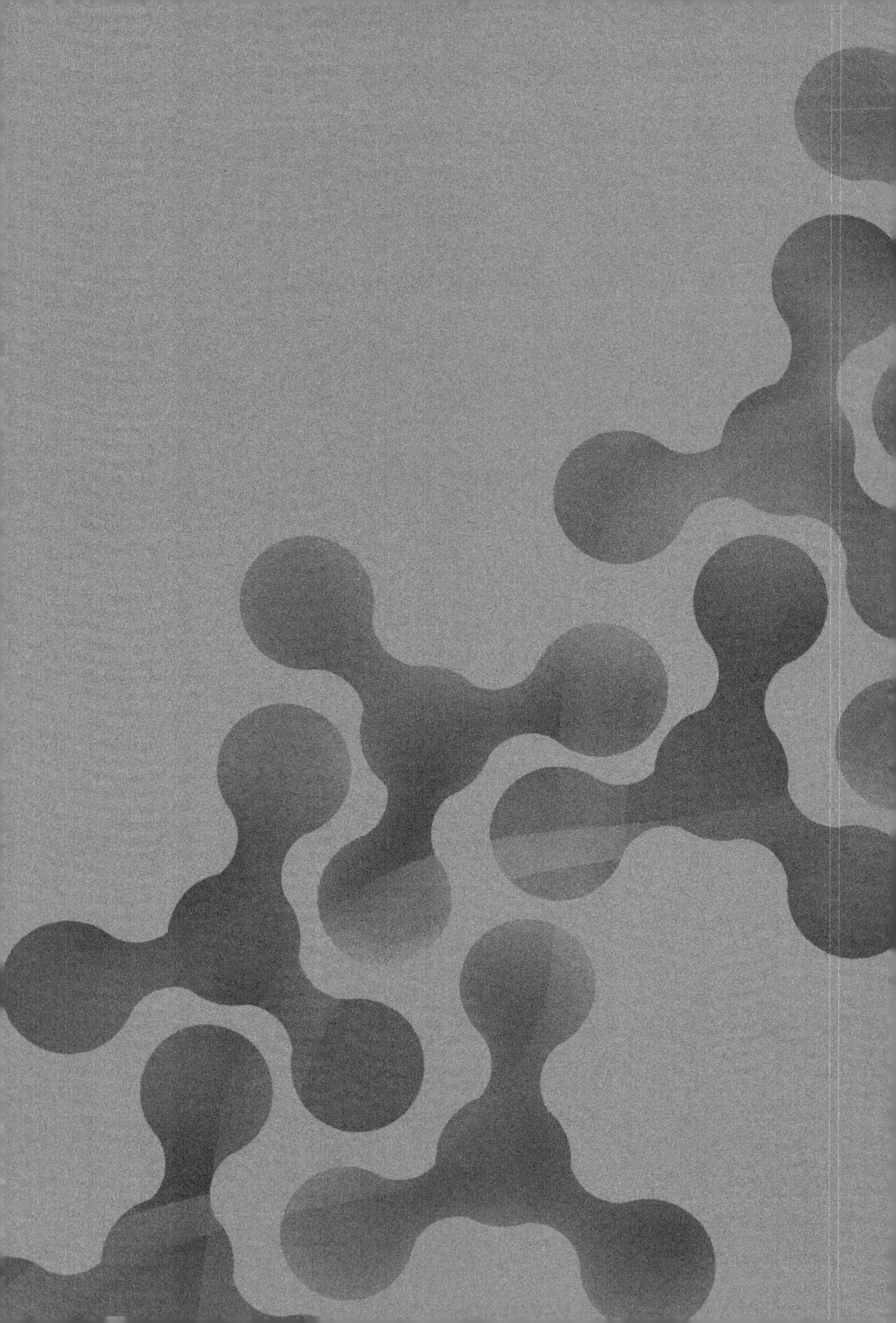

1. Introduction

IPMA has been using the IPMA Project Excellence Model (IPMA PEM) for the assessment of projects in the annual IPMA Global Project Excellence Award competition since 2002, evaluating projects from different sectors and from different geographical regions, according to a standardised methodology and process. The IPMA PEM was originally published by the German Project Management Association (GPM) in the 1990s, and was based on the Total Quality Management (TQM) approach and the EFQM model, in which evidence of good management has an equal weight to evidence of results, and in which only results that are achieved through a conscious management effort can be scored.

The IPMA PEM is a proven model for assessing and benchmarking project management, project results and their interdependencies, even though it does not claim to be founded on a scientifically proven basis for project excellence. The experience gathered from the IPMA Global Project Excellence Awards process (since 2002) demonstrates a clear link between successful projects and having well-established project management practices in place.

After more than 20 years, it was time to update the IPMA PEM to reflect new trends in project management, where factors such as sustainability and the environment are now much more relevant. For these reasons, IPMA decided not only to update the IPMA PEM, but also to create the IPMA Project Excellence Baseline® (IPMA PEB) of which the IPMA PEM is an essential part.

The purpose of the IPMA PEB is to define and explain the model, its use, its context and the underlying management philosophy (see Figure 1-1).

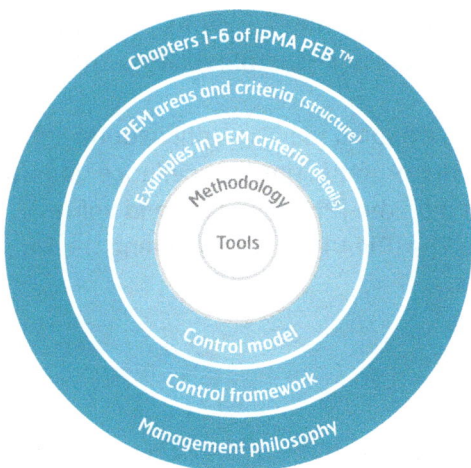

Figure 1-1: IPMA PEB as a driver for project management approach, control framework and/or control model

The IPMA PEB adds a contextual framework around the IPMA PEM, while the excellence model itself continues to deliver a structure and framework of areas to consider when assessing or controlling the perceived level of project excellence. Through elaboration of detailed sub-criteria, as well as a methodology, processes and tools to assess a project, the IPMA PEM can be used as a benchmarking model to measure the level of project excellence on a scale from 0-100%.

The body of the IPMA PEB (Chapters 2–6) describes the broader context of project excellence and provides a guideline for the overall assessment process. It is complemented by Annex A, which describes the IPMA PEM itself. Annex B provides the scoring tables used to assess project excellence and in Annex C, a general description of the assessment process implemented in the IPMA Global Project Excellence Award competition is given.

Chapter 2 describes the purpose of the IPMA PEB and its intended users, as well as the many ways it can be used. It is for each user to decide how to use the IPMA PEB. For example, the application of the IPMA PEB at the start of a project may inspire the adoption of principles that could contribute to project excellence during realisation. It can also be used as a standard for self-assessment during or after a project to determine the extent to which the project management approach translates to excellent project results. In addition, the IPMA PEB is the framework for external assessments and benchmarks (e.g. through the IPMA Global Project Excellence Awards), to receive additional independent perspectives and benchmarking information, enabling a comparison at a global level of excellence across different industries, or within the organisation itself.

Chapter 3 defines a project in its larger context, ranging from a narrow perspective (for instance as part of a programme or portfolio inside an organisational frame) to a wider perspective, for instance in relation to its external environment. In these perspectives, the topic of sustainability is introduced as a relevant part of project excellence. Sustainability is specifically addressed in Chapter 4.4.

Chapter 4 defines and explains the IPMA philosophy behind project excellence. Moving away from the organisational excellence definition of EFQM, the IPMA PEM is directly based on the IPMA concept and values.

Chapter 5 introduces the IPMA PEM by explaining the three basic building blocks of which it consists:
1. People & Purpose;
2. Processes & Resources;
3. Project Results.

For a reader who is familiar with the IPMA PEM used from 1996 to 2015, the main difference is that the enabler criteria (previously the five Project Management criteria) are now divided into two blocks separating People & Purpose from Processes & Resources (consisting of 3 and 2 sub-criteria respectively). This creates a clearer distinction between the human and non-human factors within project management. An equally fundamental change is to present and approach the criteria as interactive entities that are interdependent and can be combined in a more interactive and fluid way.

Finally, Chapter 6 introduces the principles of the assessment of project excellence before introducing the IPMA PEM in Annex A as well as the scoring tables (Annex B) and the IPMA Global Project Excellence Award assessment process (Annex C).

1.1. IPMA PEB links to IPMA OCB and IPMA ICB

The three IPMA standards — IPMA Individual Competence Baseline (IPMA ICB®), IPMA Project Excellence Baseline® (IPMA PEB) and IPMA Organisational Competence Baseline (IPMA OCB®) are complementary and provide the baseline for excellence from an individual, project and/or organisational perspective respectively. In addition to the IPMA PEB, the IPMA ICB provides a definition and overview of the competences expected from project management personnel; the IPMA OCB addresses the ability of organisations to integrate and align people, resources, processes, structures and cultures in projects, programmes and portfolios within a supporting governance and management system.

Projects rely on people with their individual competences, but the presence of competent people in the project team alone is not a guarantee for success. Projects depend on organisational support, but project failure could happen even in organisations with highly competent project managers.

Only project leaders and teams that are able to clearly define the project objectives, align stakeholder needs, develop effective teams with necessary competences, adjust and integrate processes in their project and achieve results that lead to the satisfaction of all project participants and key stakeholders are considered to be excellent. The IPMA PEB draws upon the concepts of individual and organisational competences in project management (IPMA ICB and IPMA OCB) but focuses only on how all factors come together in a specific and concrete project, allowing the level of project excellence to be measured.

The IPMA Delta® assessment, which measures organisational competence to support projects, draws simultaneously on the IPMA PEB, IPMA ICB and IPMA OCB. An organisation preparing for an IPMA Delta assessment will undertake a self-assessment using both the IPMA PEB for projects and the IPMA ICB for individuals involved in projects, followed by an external assessment against the IPMA OCB.

2. Purposes and intended users

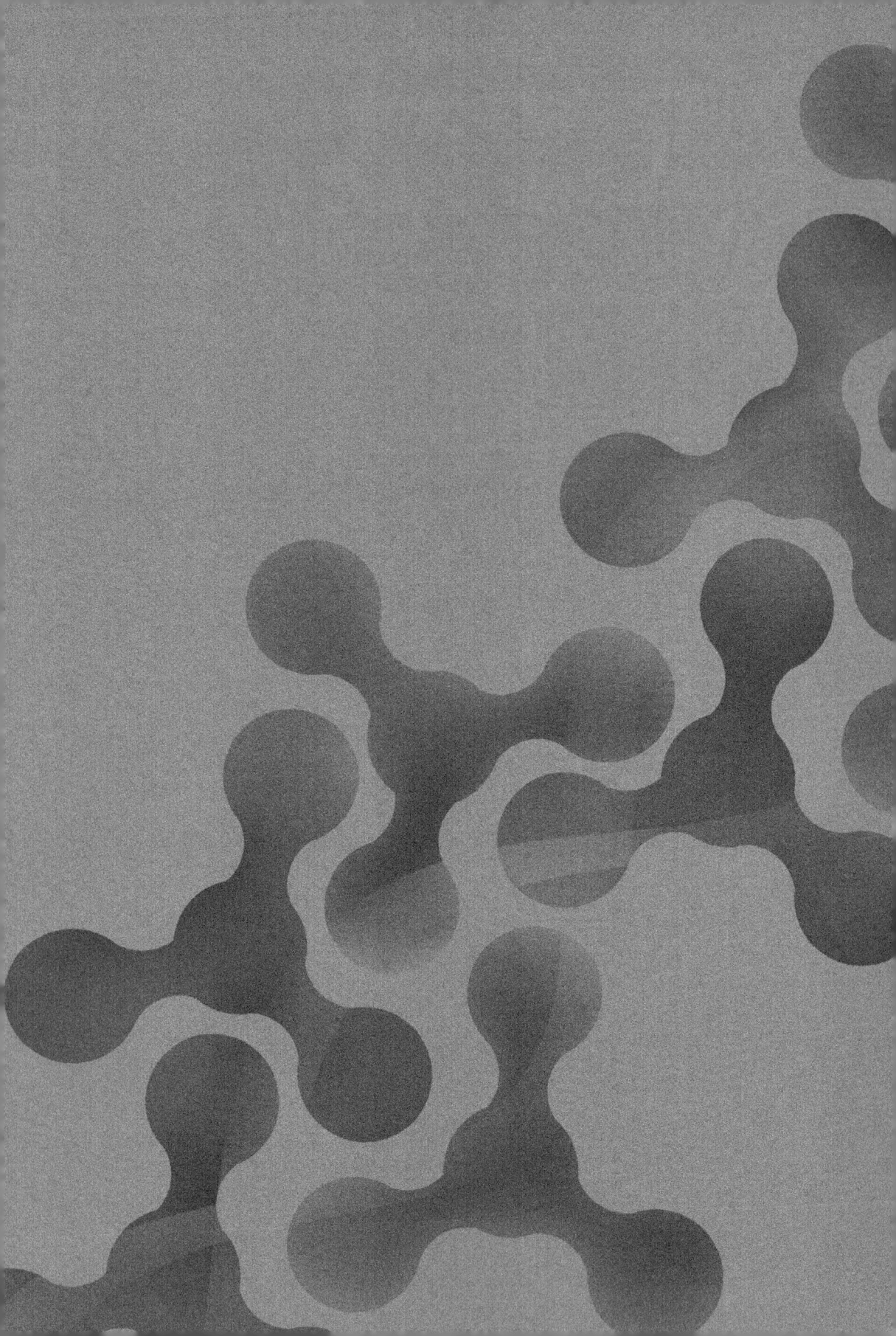

2. Purposes and intended users

2.1. Purpose of the IPMA Project Excellence Baseline

The IPMA Project Excellence Baseline® (IPMA PEB) was developed by an international community of project, programme and portfolio management experts and researchers, with a broad range of experience from different organisations, sectors and countries. The main purpose of this document is to describe the concept of excellence in managing projects and how this can help to deliver an excellent project with respect to the mission, vision and strategy.

The approach in this baseline is generic and applies to all types of projects, regardless of the context of the specific industry, sector or project management approach. It can be applied directly to programmes at the programme and/or individual project level. It is for the user to decide how this baseline can be applied and how it can be tailored to meet the needs of a specific project or programme. The IPMA PEB is a guideline providing a general understanding for people involved in project, programme and portfolio management striving for project excellence. It can be used as a measuring tool, as well as an improvement tool to analyse, monitor, develop, improve, assess and benchmark project management. It can also be used to educate, train and coach project team leaders interested in developing project excellence skills.

2.2. Typical user groups of the IPMA PEB

Given the nature of this baseline, it should be noted that there might be a multitude of different user groups interested in the application of the IPMA PEB regardless of whether they are mentioned here. The six most typical user groups identified are:
- Senior management;
- Project, programme and portfolio managers, heads/managers of project management offices(PMOs) and portfolio management offices (PfMOs);
- Knowledge, quality and process managers;
- Researchers and educators (teachers, trainers);
- IPMA Global Project Excellence Award trainers and assessors;
- Consultants.

The **senior management** of an organisation could use this baseline to understand the concept of project excellence for managing the project objectives and strategy. It can help them understand their own role and responsibilities in terms of managing an excellent project, to analyse the status of their own and the project management competences in managing excellent projects and to identify areas for improvement. In addition, it can help them gain a better understanding of the context and project environment (with stakeholders, resources and activities) necessary for the development of an excellent project. Senior managers could also use IPMA PEB as a basis for internal project assessments and benchmarking activities or to engage external partners for assessment and benchmarking purposes.

Project, programme and portfolio managers and heads/managers of PMOs and PfMOs responsible for project management activities could use the baseline in a similar way to senior management. As they are directly involved or responsible for a project, they are likely to better understand and be responsible for the implementation of IPMA PEB principles and addressing requirements for change (e.g. resulting from self-assessments or external assessment/benchmarking activities). They need to ensure that the project management continually supports project objectives and strategy; that necessary project processes and resources to achieve excellence are in place and that intended project results are achieved in order to reach project excellence. The baseline could help project managers to interact more efficiently with internal stakeholders (such as senior management) as well as with external stakeholders in order to realise their project results.

The baseline also provides the context in which project managers operate and which they need to take into account while managing their project, programme or portfolio, by developing their understanding of project excellence and of what their role and responsibilities are in achieving this excellence.

The baseline will also help project managers understand how to implement recommendations for improvements, offering a reference to improve their project or programme.

Knowledge, quality and process managers could use this baseline to provide a 360° view of projects within the organisation, taking into account: process tailoring and associated efficiency, satisfaction of stakeholders and the achieved results. Information gathered through IPMA PEB assessments can be used for process improvements, capitalisation on innovations and new knowledge gathered from projects managed by the organisation.

Researchers and educators (teachers, trainers) can use the IPMA PEB as a basis for supporting research proposals, developing project excellence competences and defining the elements of an excellent project. For this purpose, training programmes should focus on the concept of project excellence, the project excellence principles and how these can be applied in projects. Training courses should also focus on the contributions necessary from the project team members to achieve project excellence.

IPMA Global Project Excellence Award trainers and assessors can use the IPMA Project Excellence Model (IMPA PEM) to assess the project management of a project or projects that aspire to compete in the annual IPMA Global Project Excellence Awards at a global, regional or national level. These award competitions focus on identifying excellent projects in various categories (see www.ipma.world/individuals www.ipma.world/projects). The awards trainers train assessors in the application of the IPMA PEM and the execution of the project excellence awards process, as well as identifying strengths and areas for improvement in the nine criteria defined in the IPMA PEM.

Consultants, both internal and external, can use the baseline to provide consultancy to an organisation's senior managers, project managers and staff to develop the project management competences necessary for managing excellent projects. Consultants may offer benefits such as specific expertise in a certain relevant project management or results area, an independent view and additional knowledge capacity. They could also provide services such as carrying out or contributing to assessments, training, mentoring and coaching. In addition, the baseline can be used as a reference for conducting an assessment, finding areas for improvement and contributing to the sustainable development of a project, programme or portfolio.

3. The project in its context

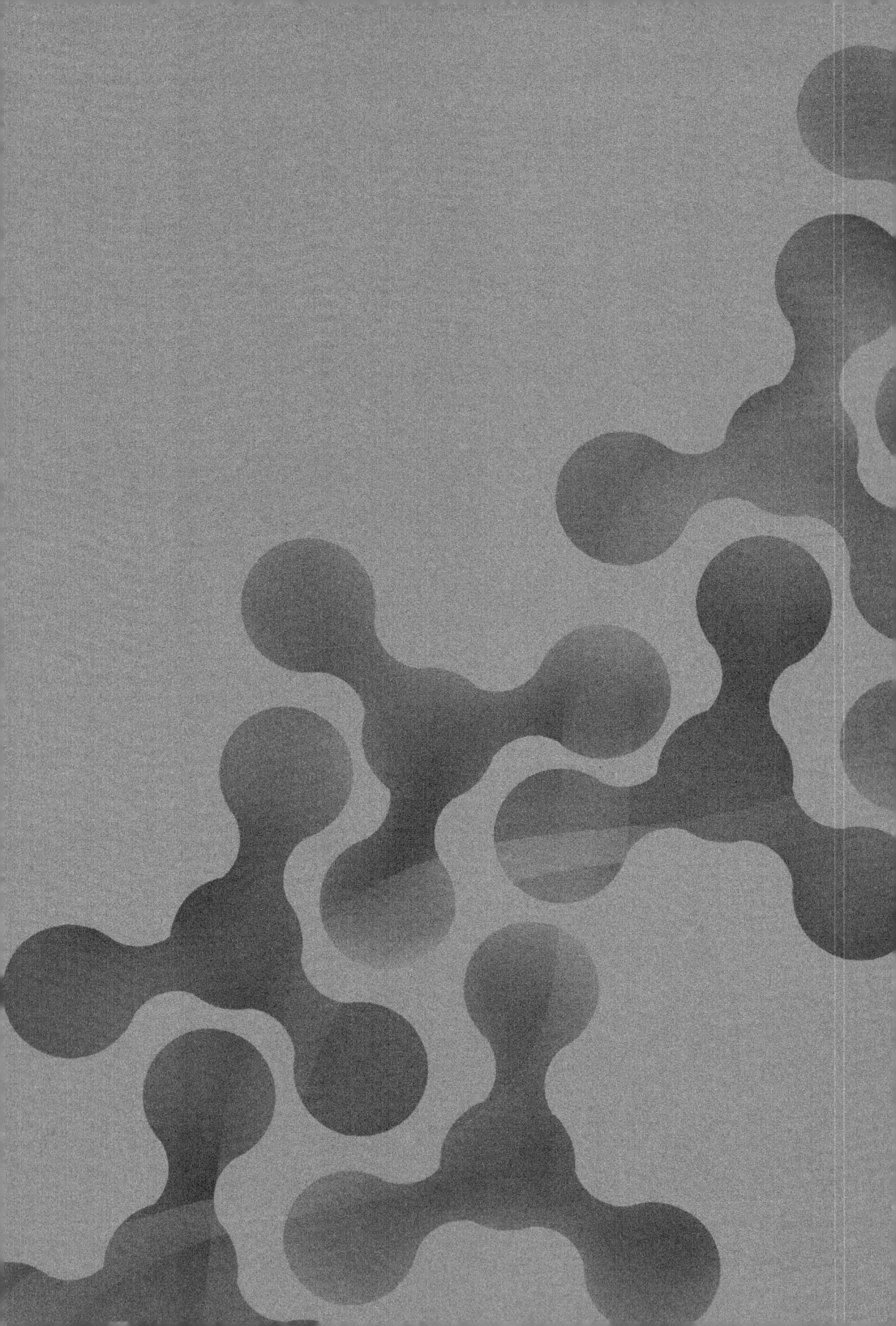

3. The project in its context

This chapter describes the project as a temporary organisation. It discusses specific tasks and challenges faced by project leaders and teams in managing their projects in their internal and external context.

3.1. What is a project?

3.1.1. The project in an organisation

In both private and public sector organisations, activities are increasingly set up and managed as projects. Organisations deal with projects in areas including information and communication technology, organisational development, product development, marketing changes, research, events, political projects, educational projects and social projects. The list is endless.

Numerous project management methodologies and tools have been developed and implemented in organisations to manage these different types of project. However, the number of failed projects is still high. Projects are over budget, run over schedule and/or do not deliver the required quality. Analyses of the causes of failure show a range of issues, including very basic ones such as a lack of understanding of the project goals or lack of strategic alignment. Other common issues are insufficient stakeholder engagement, lack of leadership, poor team organisation or poor processes.

For this reason, it is important to carry out regular analyse of project management performance to define critical success factors and promote good practices. The IPMA PEB provides a concept and the tools to achieve this and to enable a process of continuous improvement in the project.

A project is defined as a 'unique, temporary, multidisciplinary and organised endeavour to realise agreed deliverables within pre-defined requirements and constraints' (IPMA ICB). Project success is defined by IPMA as 'the appreciation of the project outcomes by the various interested parties'. This definition is more challenging than simply 'to produce the project deliverables within time and budget'.

The IPMA Organisational Competence Baseline (IPMA OCB®) defines projects as a means for implementing organisational strategies and proposes the Balanced Scorecard as a tool for 'translating' the strategic goals from strategy to the project perspective. It is important at the end of a project to analyse whether the project outputs heve met the stated objectives as perceived by the stakeholders. Other checks may verify whether the project delivered outputs in the most efficient way using scarce resources effectively.

3.1.2. The project as a temporary organisation

ISO 21500 differentiates projects from operations by stating that projects are performed by temporary teams, are non-repetitive and provide unique deliverables. Project management differs from other management disciplines because of the temporary and unique nature of projects. Temporary means that the project has a defined beginning and end in time, and therefore defined scope and resources.

The following are the most significant differences between projects and 'business-as-usual':
- Projects are unique and specific. In principle, all elements that are predetermined in a business process need to be defined specifically for a project, including tasks, conditions, rules and logic of the process flow;
- A dedicated project organisation needs to be established, either as a part of or in addition to the existing permanent organisation, or even as a new, separate legal entity;
- Employees from the line organisation may be assigned to work on a full-time or part-time basis in a project, for example following the matrix organisation approach, where staff members work and report to the project (technical, project-related) and to the department (technical and hierarchical) in parallel;
- Project team members often do not know each other at the beginning of the project, especially in unique projects or large organisations;
- The project team needs to develop its own culture and management approach – working relationships and project-specific internal procedures and guidelines that differ from those of the permanent organisation.

The temporary project organisation has its own rules, procedures, roles, communication and reporting structures, which can be set up quickly, then dismantled quickly after project results have been achieved.

In a fast-changing society, it will be increasingly difficult to define an organisation, because of the constant need for organisations to change, and to be flexible enough to adapt to changing resources and problems. In this logic, and with an internet-based society, a project becomes a temporary 'social network' of stakeholders that aims to deliver particular benefits.

In this social network, each stakeholder (a node of the network) actively joins the project. This is different from the way organisations might traditionally view stakeholders, where they were basically seen as a resource with a passive role.

For this reason, as part of the IPMA PEM update, it was decided to focus on the suppliers and contractors from the people perspective. Previously, they had been seen as a resource, but this was found to be outdated, as all the IPMA Global Project Excellence Award winners from recent years have consistently applied a 'one team' approach, where project success comes through the integration of the project team beyond organisational borders.

The IPMA OCB applies the concept of competences to groups of people (e.g. project teams and organisations). It states that the competence of the team is much higher than the collective competences of its individuals. The coherence of that group, with all the dynamic interactions between members and relevant stakeholders, constitutes a social system. It is an important task for a project leader to build the team with the necessary levels of competence. In this respect, a project is a social system with its own team competence.

3.1.3. Processes in a project

ISO 21500 defines a project as a unique set of processes consisting of coordinated and controlled activities with a start and end date, performed to achieve project objectives. The following three major types of project processes are defined in the international standard:
- Project management processes, which are specific to project management and determine how the activities selected for the project are managed;
- Delivery processes, which result in the specification and provision of a particular product, service or result and which vary depending on the particular industry and type of project deliverable (e.g. design, construction, commissioning etc.);
- Support processes, which provide relevant and valuable support to product and project management processes (e.g. logistics, accounting, safety, HR etc.).

The project leader and project team should identify processes needed for performing the project, check the resource availability, acquire and align them.

3.2. A project in its external context

The project environment may impact the project performance and its success. ISO 21500 defines factors of the project environment that the project team should consider (see Figure 3-1) for the external vs. internal project context):
- Factors outside the organisational boundary, such as socio-economic, geographical, political, regulatory, technological and ecological;
- Factors inside the organisational boundary, such as strategy, technology, project management maturity, resource availability, organisational culture and structure.

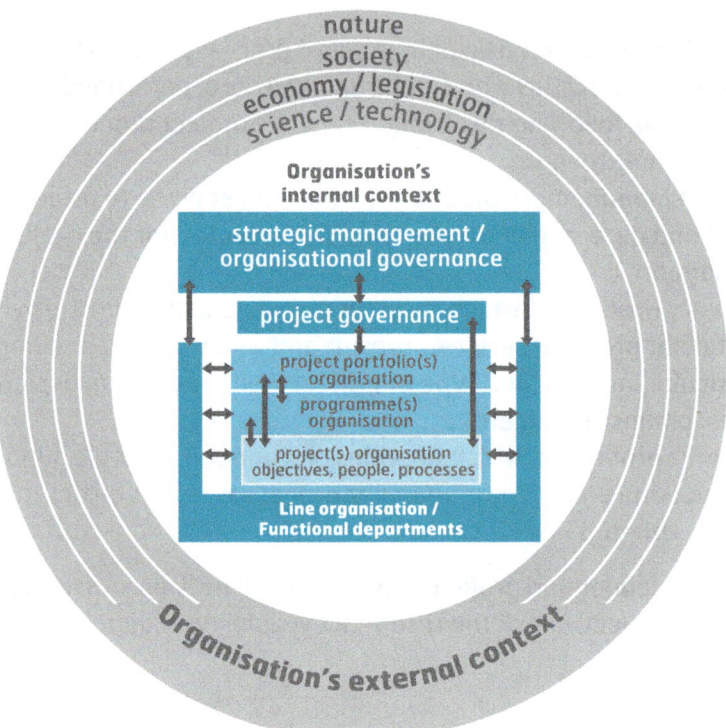

Figure 3-1: External versus internal project context

According to ISO 21500 '...factors outside the organisational boundary may have an impact on the project by imposing constraints or introducing risks affecting the project. Although these factors are often beyond the control of the project manager, they should still be considered'.

Projects often use resources and produce outputs that may influence the environment. Project leaders and project teams should take responsibility for sustainability, i.e. improving the quality of human life, while living within the carrying capacity of the supporting eco-systems. In the IPMA PEM, the integration of sustainable development concepts into all aspects of project management is considered essential, which should ensure that a balance is achieved between economic goals, social sustainability and environmental sustainability.

Following the principles of sustainability, the IPMA PEM takes into account the fact that, in some cases, this is likely to increase the number of stakeholders considered by the project. For example, the interests of local communities, environmental protection and the views of other non-governmental organisations should be taken into consideration.

Projects are impacted by a number of political, social and technological factors. These may provide additional constraints and should be considered by the project leader and the project team. For example, project management activities should be adjusted according to laws and regulations, which may apply in a specific country or industry.

The more internal and external factors influencing a project, the higher the complexity of the project and the greater the requirement for a complex project management system.

3.3. A project in its organisational context

3.3.1. Organisational context

A project is usually executed as an activity of a permanent (parent) organisation. There are relationships between the project and its organisational context. Project activities could be linked with pre-project and post-project activities such as business case development or transition to operations or maintenance.

Projects (and programmes) are temporary organisations. Standardised project management processes and value-added processes that are necessary for the realisation of the project exist in many organisations. Even though these processes often significantly accelerate the
planning of the project, they have to be adapted to the specific characteristics of a project before it is executed.

The project organisation is team-based and unites people from different areas of an organisation (e.g. sales, development, production, marketing, IT) for the provision of new, interdisciplinary and often complex tasks. It uses reporting and decision-making processes that have been established specifically for the project. Project staff are usually allocated for the duration of the project to an agreed proportion of working time and according to established organisational rules. A clear definition of roles and responsibilities, both in the project and the line organisation, is an important prerequisite for efficient operations, enabling the project staff to complete their tasks effectively. Organisations introducing projects should execute the necessary organisational adjustments to align the project and the line organisation. If this is not done properly, it could cause conflicts between the project and the line organisation while they are performing their different roles.

The organisational structure, culture, systems and processes affect project processes, project team organisation and culture. The project management approach that works in one organisation may not work efficiently in every organisation and for every project.

3.3.2. Project governance

The IPMA OCB specifies governance as another key function to be considered in project, programme and portfolio management. Organisational governance consists of the framework and principles by which an organisation is directed and regulated. Project governance, as defined in ISO 21500, 'includes, but is not limited to, those areas of organisational governance that are specifically related to project activities'. Project governance could define organisational policies, processes and methodologies to be used in projects, the management structure, limits of authority for decision-making, etc. One of the IPMA PEM principles is that project leaders and the project team align their activities with principles and policies defined by the project governance.

3.3.3. The project in the context of a programme and portfolio

Projects are often initiated, planned and executed within an organisation's programme or portfolio.

In the IPMA ICB and IPMA OCB, a programme is defined as a 'temporary organisation of interrelated programme components (constituent initiatives) managed in a coordinated way to enable the implementation of change and the realisation of benefits'. Therefore, a programme could consist of a number of projects that are designed to provide benefits and outcomes on a strategic level. It is more than the sum of all projects and their deliverables. Programmes are also managed as a temporary organisation and use project and programme management methodologies.

A portfolio is defined as a 'set of projects and/or programmes, which are not necessarily related, brought together to provide for optimum use of the organisation's resources and to achieve the organisation's strategic goals while minimising the level of portfolio risk'. Portfolio management is a permanent operation and is about the centralised management of processes, methods, and technologies used in an organisation to analyse and manage current or proposed projects based on key characteristics. The objectives are to select the most appropriate programmes and projects from all proposed initiatives; determine the optimal resource mix for delivery and to schedule activities to achieve the organisational strategic, operational and financial goals, while observing constraints imposed by stakeholders and other internal or external factors.

Project objectives should be aligned with the organisational strategy, programme goals and KPIs. Project management processes should be aligned with the programme and project portfolio structures and processes.

The IPMA PEB can be applied to projects and programmes as temporary organisations but is not meant to be applied to portfolios. This is because there are significant differences between the nature and purpose of portfolio management and project management processes.

4. Introducing project excellence

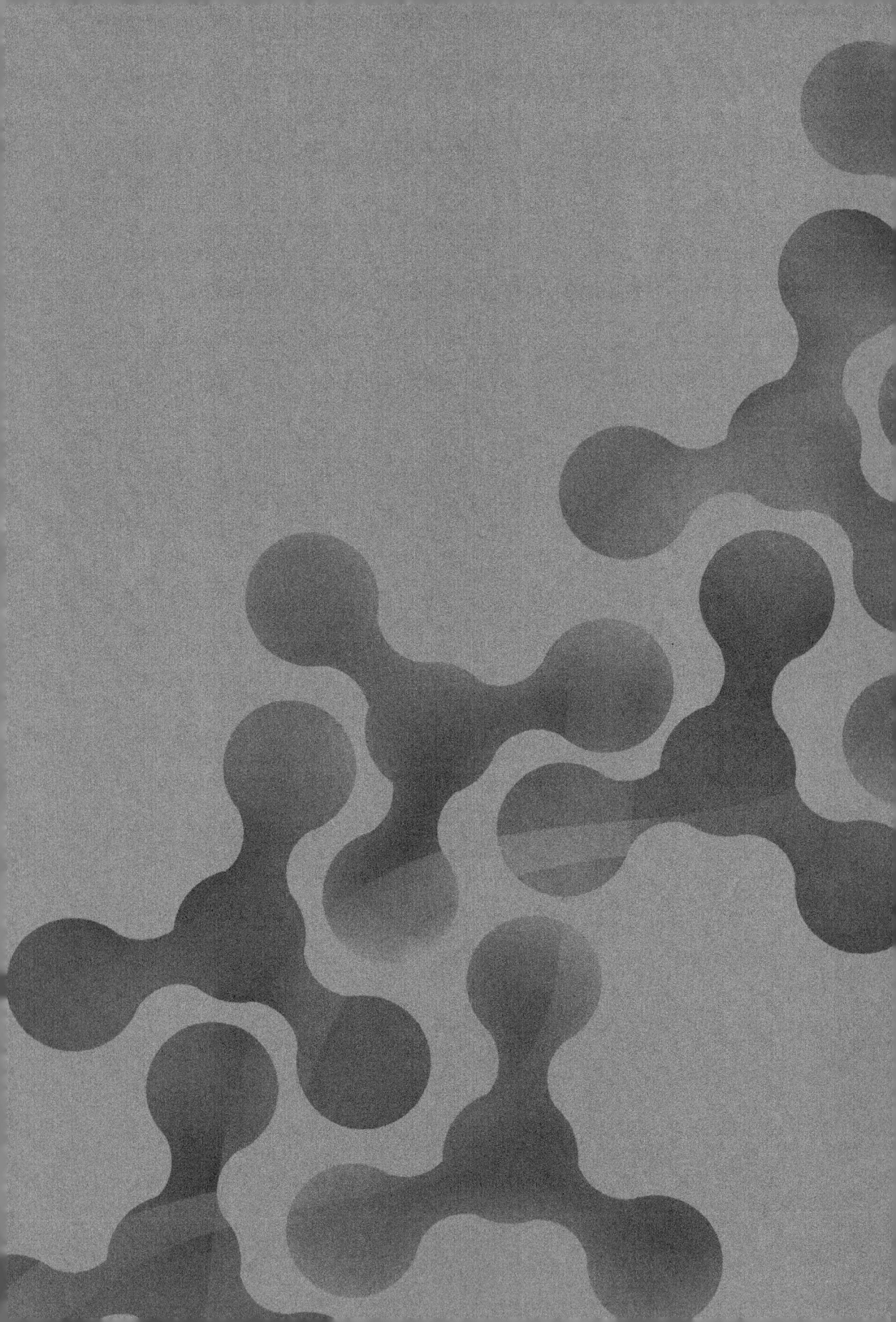

4. Introducing project excellence

4.1. The concept of excellence

Ancient Greek writers had a concept of excellence (arete) as an outstanding fitness. Excellence is commonly understood as a talent or quality that is unusually good. It is also used as a standard of performance, as measured, for example, through economic indicators. Studies have shown that the most important way to achieve excellent performance is to practise.

Basic principles of excellence are:
- Excellence is a quality that surpasses ordinary standards;
- Excellence is a continuously moving target; it can never be fully reached, and there will always be room for improvement and development;
- The most important way to achieve excellent performance is to practise and continuously learn and improve in all relevant areas;
- Achieving excellence is not a short-term concept. It requires dedication and long-term efforts. It results in capabilities of an organisation that cannot be copied easily and provides a competitive advantage.

4.2. The concept of project excellence

IPMA's mission is to promote the recognition of project management and engage stakeholders around the world in advancing the project management discipline. This is reflected by the IPMA Project Excellence Model (IPMA PEM) as an assessment tool and the IPMA International Project Excellence Awards as a platform to promote role models for project excellence by rewarding excellent performance in project management. It facilitates the identification and spread of new and brilliant approaches to project management that have a proven link to project success.

Project excellence is a set of characteristics that has been demonstrated in actual projects. Due to the nature of the developments and innovations in the project management field, it is not and will never be a clearly defined, prescriptive collection of approaches, methods or practices.

Excellent projects must demonstrate excellent performance in all project management aspects, including the management of people, purpose, processes, resources and results. Results are only credited insofar as they are a consequence of leadership and management processes. Excellent projects apply the approaches and methods of project management in professional and innovative ways, reflecting on their own approach, methodologies and results in order to learn from them and taking actions for improvement when necessary.

Excellent projects often experience the need to develop new standards, which may go beyond, or even contradict, existing standards, methods, tools or techniques, in order to respond to the needs of the project. However, such decisions are always based on a careful analysis of the situation and after considering alternative solutions.

Project excellence promotes the use of research, experiments and other means in order to bring innovation to the way a project is managed. However, the main focus is on the successful management of the actual project and the results.

The professional community can learn from excellent projects, enrich their knowledge and ideally benefit from project management as a discipline.

Excellent projects lead to added value beyond the actual project goals, thereby enriching businesses, societies, the environment, etc.

4.3. Continuous improvement as a foundation for excellence

When working towards project excellence, the emphasis should be on continuous improvement and constant learning. The continuous improvement principle is in line with the Deming (PDCA) cycle (see Figure 4-1).

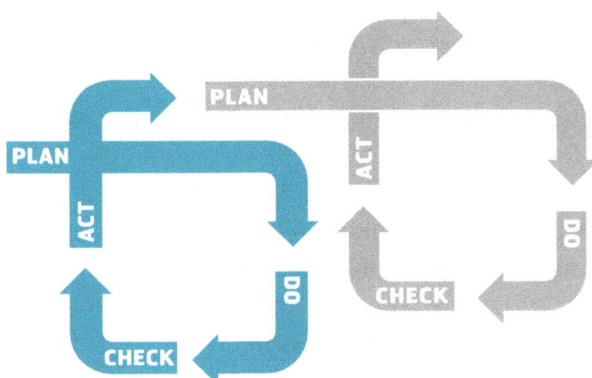

Figure 4-1: The use of the PDCA cycle of continuous improvement

Project managers looking to introduce excellence into their projects will develop and systematically adapt their project management approach from the principle of continuous improvement and learning.

In principle this continuous improvement and learning cycle follows an iterative, four-step management method:

- **Plan:** In the start-up phase of the project, the project team selects procedures, methods, approaches and tools that are appropriate to plan, execute, monitor and control the project and reflect the complexity of the project. Sources considered by the team may include industry or company management standards, specific definitions of processes or process elements created for the project, etc. In cases where the standards do not suit the requirements of the project, the team adapts them or develops project-specific procedures, methods, approaches and tools.
- **Do:** The project team implements the selected procedures, methods, approaches and tools in the actual project and makes use of them.
- **Check:** The project team regularly evaluates the procedures, methods, approaches and tools used in the project to determine whether they are (still) appropriate and optimal for managing the project and whether they lead to expected results and/or need to be improved.

- **Act:** Based on these evaluations, the project team analyses and prioritises the findings and agrees on the activities to be planned and executed to improve the project management approach.

Based on this input, the PDCA cycle starts again:
- **Plan:** Based on the input from the previous cycle, the project team improves those procedures, methods, approaches and tools where potential for improvement has been identified, or develops appropriate new ap-
proaches (e.g. a new procurement process for capital goods with long lead times);
- **Do:** The project team implements the modified or new procedures, metods,
approaches and tools in the actual project and makes use of them;
- **Check:** The project team regularly evaluates the established/modified/new procedures, methods, approaches and tools used in the project to determine whether they are appropriate and optimal for managing the project and whether they lead to expected results and/or need to be improved;
- **Act:** Based on these evaluations, the project team analyses and prioritises the findings and agrees on the activities to be planned and executed to improve the project management approach.

Based on this input, the PDCA cycle continues.

The PDCA approach leads to a process of continuous improvement in the management of projects and enables the project team to achieve benefits (as described in Chapter 5.5) and strive for excellence.

4.4. The role of sustainability

The integration of sustainability principles and objectives into projects commences well before a project starts, so that the long-term benefits are identified, addressed and integrated into the project management. An important part of integrating sustainable principles and objectives into projects is the alignment of the project and its team(s) to organisational objectives and reporting.

The UN Global Compact's Ten Principles of Sustainability [5] are in the areas of human rights, labour, the environment and anti-corruption. These principles are derived from:
- The Universal Declaration of Human Rights;
- The International Labour Organisation's Declaration on Fundamental Principles and Rights at Work;
- The Rio Declaration on Environment and Development;
- The United Nations Convention Against Corruption.

The UN Global Compact asks companies to embrace, support and enact, within their sphere of influence, a set of core values in the areas of human rights, labour standards, the environment and anti-corruption. In the IPMA Project Excellence Baseline® (IPMA PEB), projects are asked to make similar contributions within the project context and areas of influence.

Sustainability is now recognised as a global driver and the beginning of a collaborative, system approach to sustainability, positively creating value for organisations [6]. As an expression of an organisation's strategy, projects of any type are perfectly positioned to deliver value and long-term benefits at many levels.

The three pillars of sustainability, identified at the 2005 World Summit on Social Development, are economic development, social development and environmental protection. These three pillars are not mutually exclusive and they can reinforce each other, as they have served as a common ground for numerous sustainability standards and certification systems including ISO 26000 (Corporate Social Responsibility), the Rainforest Alliance and Fairtrade. Supporting standards include ISO 14063:2006 (Environment, and its related standards ISO 14001, 14004, 14006, 14064) and ISO 50001 (Energy Management Systems).

While the concept of sustainability was initially attributed to industries with the biggest impact on the natural environment, project excellence builds on the idea that sustainability can be applied to any project.

Leaders of excellent projects have a responsibility to ensure that the impact of the project from a sustainability perspective is recognised and actively managed to deliver sustainable outcomes.

In practice, leaders of excellent projects:
- Behave in a socially responsible way, taking care of stakeholders with limited power who are impacted by the project;
- Understand the key elements of the project environment, including, but not limited to, the natural environment, social systems and the economy;
- Whenever applicable, recognise environmental bodies and organisations as project stakeholders and cooperate with them.

Therefore, when setting objectives, the project is expected to ensure that it clearly addresses sustainability as described by the ten principles and three pillars described above. Furthermore, where applicable, the project is expected to identify and implement additional project management processes, tools, methodologies, structures and resources for managing areas such as:
- Security and safety;
- Social responsibility;
- Environmental protection;
- Appropriate sustainability monitoring and controls;
- Performance and reporting.

Every excellent organisation needs to understand that optimal decisions cannot be taken in isolation from the environment. Ethics and social responsibility play an important role in all decisions and the challenge is to understand the widest possible environment and the long-term view and then refine the scope to what is practical and feasible to achieve, as well as monitor and control all these criteria during the project implementation.

The Global Reporting Initiative (GRI) drives sustainability reporting and produces a comprehensive Sustainability Reporting Framework that is widely used around the world, to enable greater organisational transparency. This framework, including the Sustainability Reporting Guidelines, sets up the Principles and Standard Disclosures which organisations can use to report their economic, environmental, and social performance and impacts.

In addition to the value created, the benefits of sustainability management in projects include:
- Continuous improvement and competitive advantage;
- Development of a collaborative, system approach to sustainable projects;
- Improved project controls;
- Benchmarking and assessing sustainability performance with respect to international laws, norms, codes, performance standards and voluntary initiatives;

- Demonstrating how the organisation influences and is influenced by the expectations about sustainable development;
- Comparing performance within an organisation and between different organisations over time.

Finally, the impact of this focus on sustainability and the environment should affect the visible project results in the perception of the other stakeholders (Annex A criterion C.3a.) even if it is not directly required by the customer.

4.5. The role of leadership

Genuine leaders form the culture of the organisation and steer resources and efforts towards excellent achievements. Therefore, leadership quality is imperative and authentic leadership cannot be confined to the professional environment alone. It needs to be founded on personal maturity and a lifelong interest in personal development. However, the best kind of leadership is not about a 'one size fits all' approach. It is much more a matter of adapting to the context, values, needs and expectations of the specific environment.

4.6. The link between competence and excellence

Two of the key IPMA standards, IPMA Individual Competence Baseline (IPMA ICB®) and IPMA Organisational Competence Baseline (IPMA OCB®), are built on the concept of competences for the individual and organisation respectively. The idea of project excellence supports these two standards by providing mechanisms that lead to continuous competence development throughout the lifetime of a project.

It is expected that projects assessed to be excellent according to this standard lead, to substantial improvement of both individual and organisational competences as described in IPMA ICB and IPMA OCB.

The IPMA PEM requires that the full potential of individual and organisational competences is used to achieve project success and to realise excellence. This is accomplished through a good understanding of the needs of the project and the potential of all key project stakeholders, plus the alignment of leadership styles, project strategy and processes.

The IPMA PEB not only promotes continuous adaptation based on observed results, but also requires factual evidence that competences are continuously developed and used to achieve and improve project success.

5. Introduction to the Project Excellence Model

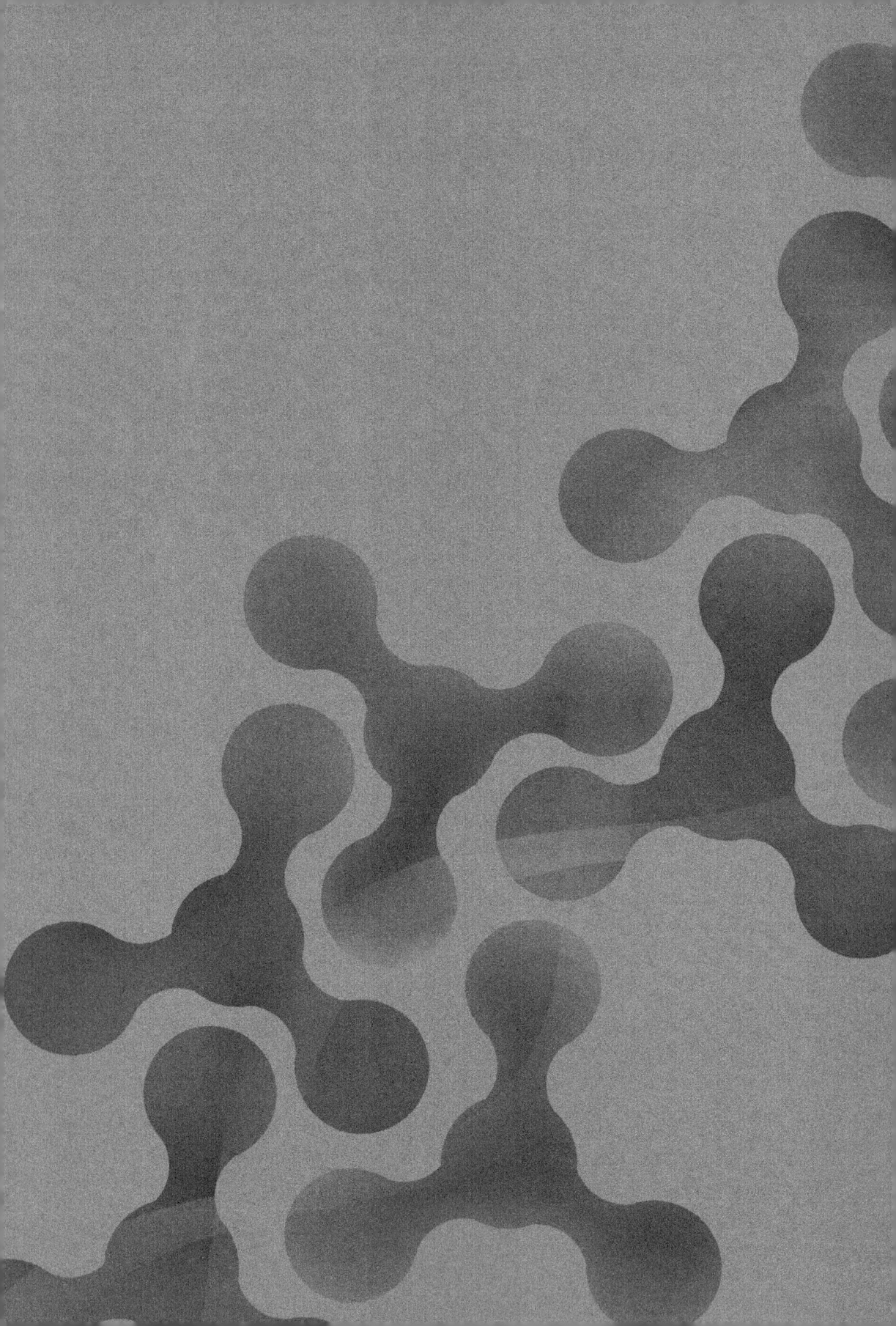

5. Introduction to the Project Excellence Model

5.1. Principles behind the model design

The main purpose of the IPMA Project Excellence Model (IPMA PEM) is to provide guidance to organisations in assessing the ability of their projects and programmes to achieve project excellence, as defined in the previous chapter. As the model is based on Total Quality Management (TQM) and related models (e.g. EFQM), organisations that have already dealt with these concepts will easily apply and use the IPMA PEM.

The IPMA PEM focuses on a project or a programme, complementing two other IPMA standards:
- **IPMA Individual Competence Baseline (IPMA ICB®)** – designed to assess the individual competences of project, programme and portfolio leaders;
- **IPMA Organisational Competence Baseline (IPMA OCB®)** – designed to assess the competences of organisations that run projects.

Used together, the three standards provide a comprehensive way to assess a project within its organisational environment.

The IPMA PEM can be used regardless of the project management approach applied to the project. The main reason for this is that the IPMA PEM does not enforce any particular approach to project decomposition, organisation or planning. It also does not suggest any particular
project management tools or techniques. The main focus is on the conscious use of the most effective management approaches and methods that lead to expected results and enable continuous improvement.

This means that the IPMA PEM can be used for assessing the implementation of project management within particular projects. It makes the IPMA PEM a good companion for well-established project management methodologies, helping to assess their fitness for use in particular project situations and to link the use of a given methodology with the achieved results.

It is worth emphasising that, due to the nature of project excellence as defined in the previous chapter, there is an assumption in the design of the model that it might not be feasible or reasonable to meet all of its criteria in full. The IPMA PEM is designed to drive continuous improvement efforts regardless of the starting conditions of the project and the outcome achieved.

5.2. Structure of the model

The basic structure of the model is simple. The model serves as a standard and offers guidelines for excellent project management regardless of the size of the project, its maturity and/or context.

The structure of the IPMA PEM enables easy reporting of the outcomes on all management levels by introducing three levels of the model:
- **Areas** – This level shows the main components of project excellence (People & Purpose, Processes & Resources and Results). The first two areas are considered to be the enablers for excellent project management and the third is the outcome of successful leadership and management. The areas enable feedback on an executive level, showing the overall state of key enablers of excellence and their actual outcome.
- **Criteria** – This level is primarily intended to enable detailed feedback about the levels of excellence on a particular project to be delivered in a structured way. It covers the key factors that make up the project excellence areas and enables measurement for development and benchmarking purposes.
- **Examples** – The third level of the IPMA PEM refers to actual practices typically found in excellent projects. Findings at this level can be used by project practitioners to improve their performance in managing projects and creating a sustainable environment for excellence. It also enables the authors of organisational methodologies to identify particular practices where methods could be enhanced and/or modified for a better alignment with project needs.

5.3. Areas of the model and interpretation of the overall results

The model is divided into the following three areas (see Figure 5-1):
- **People & Purpose** – This area is considered to be the **foundation** of project excellence. The right people, led and supported by excellent leaders, all sharing a common vision for success, are crucial to drive project improvements and help the project to go beyond the established standards.
- **Processes & Resources** – This area represents practices necessary to **reinforce** excellence through sound processes and adequate resources used in an efficient and sustainable way. It also serves as a basis for securing the outcome of innovation, turning
it into a solid starting point for another wave of improvements.
- **Project Results** – The project management approach can only be excellent if it leads to outstanding, sustainable results for all key stakeholders. This area complements the first two with necessary **proof** of excellent results as defined by the project stakeholders.

Figure 5-1: Interpretation of the model areas

These areas are inspired by and closely related to the criteria of EFQM often used for the assessment of organisational excellence (see Figure 5-2).

5 Introduction to the Project Excellence Model

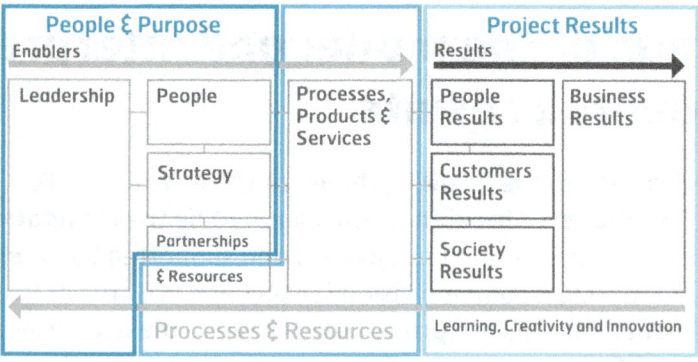

Figure 5-2: Mapping between IPMA PEM areas and EFQM criteria

This deliberate link helps organisations that use EFQM to extend their excellence efforts into projects while keeping consistency with their organisation-wide initiatives.

The results at the level of the model areas can be used to understand the overall management philosophy of the project and to make general conclusions on how the project would perform under various conditions. Examples of conclusions after assessing the level of excellence in a project could be:

Leadership driven projects with low process maturity

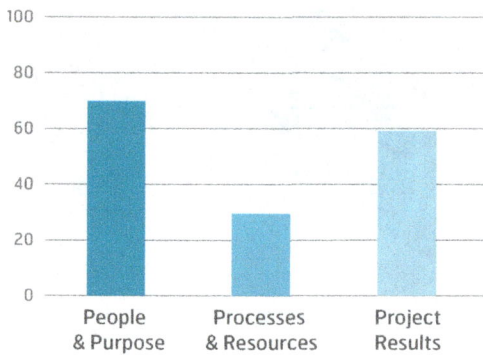

Figure 5-3: Leadership-driven project

These projects are characterised by a very strong sense of purpose and great leadership. Having highly motivated and fully dedicated teams, such projects often demonstrate a high level of flexibility and deliver great results. However, their downside is a lack of well-established management processes. Typically, this leads to a high level of unnecessary and often repeated work. In addition, these projects might have difficulties in transferring their experience and established routines effectively for the benefit of future endeavours.

Process driven projects with low leadership and/or sense of purpose

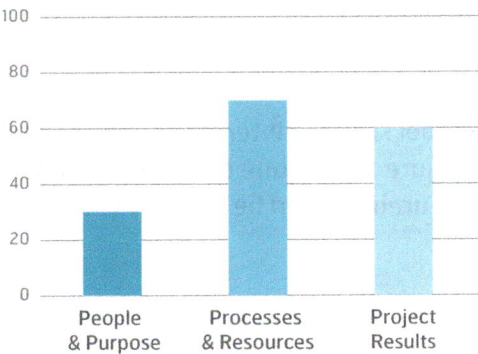

Figure 5-4: Process-driven project

Process driven projects often deliver great, repetitive results. Usually these are ensured by processes continuously improved over the years. The downside of such projects is a lack of strong leadership and/or sense of purpose. As a result, such projects are often not able to deal with disruptive changes in the environment and/or cope with significant risks.

Balanced project

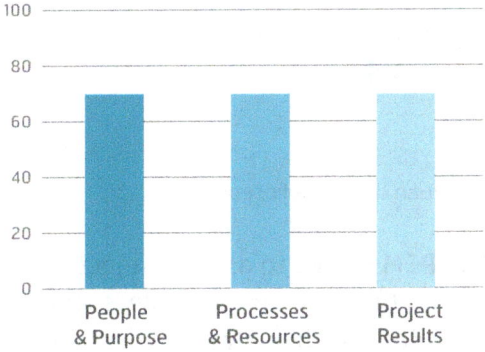

Figure 5-5: Balanced project

Balanced projects combine great leadership and a strong sense of purpose with a strong process culture. This combination ensures high levels of team motivation, flexibility and the ability to deliver great, repeatable results within and beyond a given project. Such projects prove to be able to deal with great challenges coming from political, social and technical complexities.

5.4. Interactions between the areas of the model

All three areas of the model strongly interact with each other as shown in the illustration below (see Figure 5-6). None of the areas should be developed in isolation and each of the areas should be actively used to develop excellence in the remaining two.

Figure 5-6: Interaction between the model areas

Whenever the IPMA PEM is used to assess projects or programmes, analysis of the interactions between the areas of the model should be one of the key assessment efforts. Findings from such analyses can be used to define significant improvements on a systemic level, which will fundamentally improve the ability to reach excellence.

5.5. Business value delivery using IPMA PEM

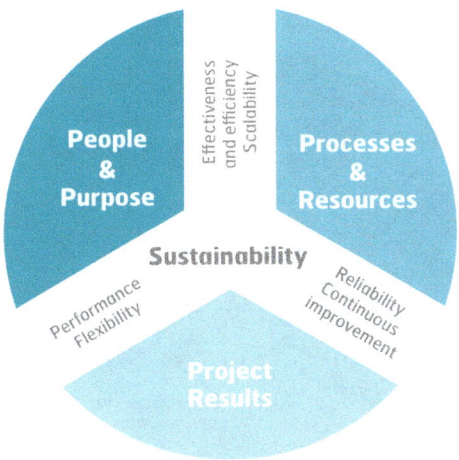

Figure 5-7: Value delivered through interaction between model areas

The following business value can be secured by ensuring close interaction between the main areas of the model (see Figure 5–7):

- **Performance** – People driven by purpose are motivated and strive to achieve results;
- **Effectiveness and efficiency** – The right processes and resources used by people driven by purpose increase their effectiveness and efficiency;
- **Reliability** – Well-established processes and adequately managed resources help to secure short – and long-term results;
- **Flexibility** – Regular observation of the results influences the perception of people and leads to a better understanding of the project objectives and continuous refinement of its strategy;
- **Continuous improvement** – Conclusions from the analysis of the results drive the development of processes and resources;
- **Scalability** – People driven by objectives look for opportunities to increase their abilities through the development and utilisation of the right processes and resources.

Sustainability, as defined in previous chapters, can be observed both in terms of effects on the environment and longevity of the results. It is achieved through continuous delivery, monitoring and use of the project results to govern the objectives, drive engagement of people, secure adequate processes and ensure responsible use of resources.

5.6. The model criteria

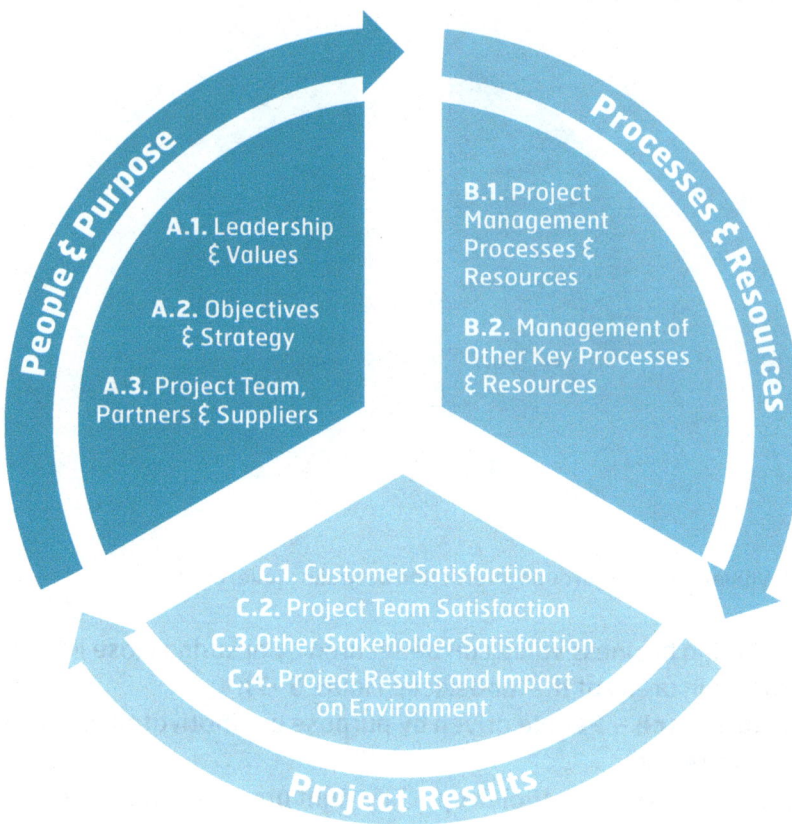

Figure 5-8: The IPMA PEM criteria

A. People & Purpose

The People & Purpose area follows the logic that project excellence starts with leaders, including sponsors, who define and follow the right values and consciously apply an effective leadership style. These leaders engage key stakeholders in the definition of the project objectives and strategy formulation. They build effective teams and engage the right partners and suppliers in order to achieve project success.

The People & Purpose area is divided into three criteria:
- (A.1.) Leadership & Values;
- (A.2.) Objectives & Strategy;
- (A.3.) Project Team, Partners & Suppliers.

(A.1.) Leadership & Values

Excellent projects are led in a way that anticipates the future and realises it with persistence. The leaders (i.e. all the people involved in a leadership/managerial role within the project or from the client/line organisation) act as role models for the project team with respect to values, morals, focus on objectives, working standards, self-management and cooperation and create a high-trust, high-inspiration environment. Leaders enable and authorise the project team to anticipate and act in time to achieve project success. They support a flexible project organisation capable of adapting to changing circumstances.

(A.2.) Objectives & Strategy

The objectives and strategies of excellent projects are defined and developed by the project leaders in alignment with stakeholders' needs and requirements. They also take into account the project environment.

Once agreed, objectives and strategies are regularly reviewed and, if necessary, adapted in response to a changing environment or to stakeholder demands.

Excellent projects use project objectives and overall project strategies to develop and continuously adapt their plans and procedures.

(A.3.) Project Team, Partners & Suppliers

In excellent projects, project team members, partners and suppliers are valued through the creation of a culture that allows the mutually beneficial achievement of organisational, project and personal goals. Fairness and equality are promoted within the project, with respect to integration and development of all involved parties.

Excellent project achievements are communicated, rewarded and recognised in a way that motivates project team members, partners and suppliers. This builds commitment and enables skills and knowledge to be used and developed in order to achieve project success.

B. Processes & Resources

The Processes & Resources area focuses on the management of the key processes contributing to project success and the resources required to realise them successfully. Given the importance of the project management processes and related resources, they receive special attention in the model. The project team should carefully select, adapt and develop them in order for the project to reach its goals in an effective and efficient way. Their adequacy for the needs of the project and its complexity should also be actively managed throughout the entire project lifecycle. However, effective and efficient project management processes alone are not sufficient conditions for project success. This is the main reason that the IPMA PEM also considers how the project team identifies other processes and resources required for project success and the way the project fits into its environment (e.g. corporate, legal, natural).

The Processes & Resources area is divided into two criteria:
    (B.1.) Project Management Processes & Resources;
    (B.2.) Management of other Key Processes & Resources.

(B.1.) Project Management Processes & Resources
Teams on excellent projects identify the key project management processes and related resources necessary for project success in cooperation with stakeholders. Key methods, tools and project management processes are selected, developed and optimised to achieve the project objectives in the most effective and efficient way. This is done based on a good understanding of the project needs and organisational capabilities.

(B.2.) Management of other Key Processes & Resources
Teams on excellent projects identify other key project delivery and support processes and related resources necessary for project success (e.g. product design, engineering, maintenance, handover and acceptance, logistics, safety and security) in cooperation with stakeholders. These methods, tools and processes are selected, developed and optimised to achieve the project objectives in the most effective and efficient way. This is achieved based on a good understanding of organisational capabilities.

C. Project Results

The Project Results area consists of criteria that provide insight into the perceptions about the management of the project held by the customer, project team members and other stakeholders, expressed in terms of their satisfaction levels, as well as indicators that prove this satisfaction level. In addition, it covers other results that can provide insight into the level of excellence achieved by the project.

Balancing the expectations and demands of all parties involved, together with great management processes, should lead to sustainable, outstanding results for all key stakeholders. The concept of sustainability as an important element of project excellence is explained specifically in Chapter 4.4 (The role of sustainability). As a fundamental principle, by definition results can only be excellent if they are also sustainable, so fully evaluating the excellence of a project entails extrapolating from the results achieved at the end of a project, in order to estimate future levels of satisfaction and success.

The Project Results area is divided into four criteria:
- (C.1.) Customer Satisfaction;
- (C.2.) Project Team Satisfaction;
- (C.3.) Other Stakeholder Satisfaction;
- (C.4.) Project Results and Impact on the Environment

(C.1.) Customer Satisfaction
Excellent projects achieve high customer satisfaction. The perceived satisfaction is consistent with the fulfilment of the project objectives, key performance indicators (quantitative and qualitative), engagement of customer representatives and their identification with the project.

In well-managed organisations and projects, the customer alone decides on the perception of quality. The customer satisfaction criterion is a reflection of how well the project team understood and fulfilled the customer needs and requirements.

(C.2.) Project Team Satisfaction
Excellent projects achieve high team member satisfaction. The perceived satisfaction is consistent with the fulfilment of the project objectives, engagement of the team members in the project and their identification with the team.

(C.3.) Other Stakeholder Satisfaction
Excellent projects achieve high stakeholder satisfaction. The perceived satisfaction is consistent with the fulfilment of the project objectives, key performance

indicators (quantitative and qualitative), engagement of the stakeholders' representatives and their identification with the project. Stakeholders representing environmental aspects of the project are highly satisfied.

(C.4.) Project Results and Impact on the Environment

Excellent projects achieve outstanding results while keeping high performance levels. Such results are achieved as an outcome of excellent management and leadership. Their positive impact on the environment is also clearly visible.

5 Introduction to the Project Excellence Model

6. Assessment of project excellence

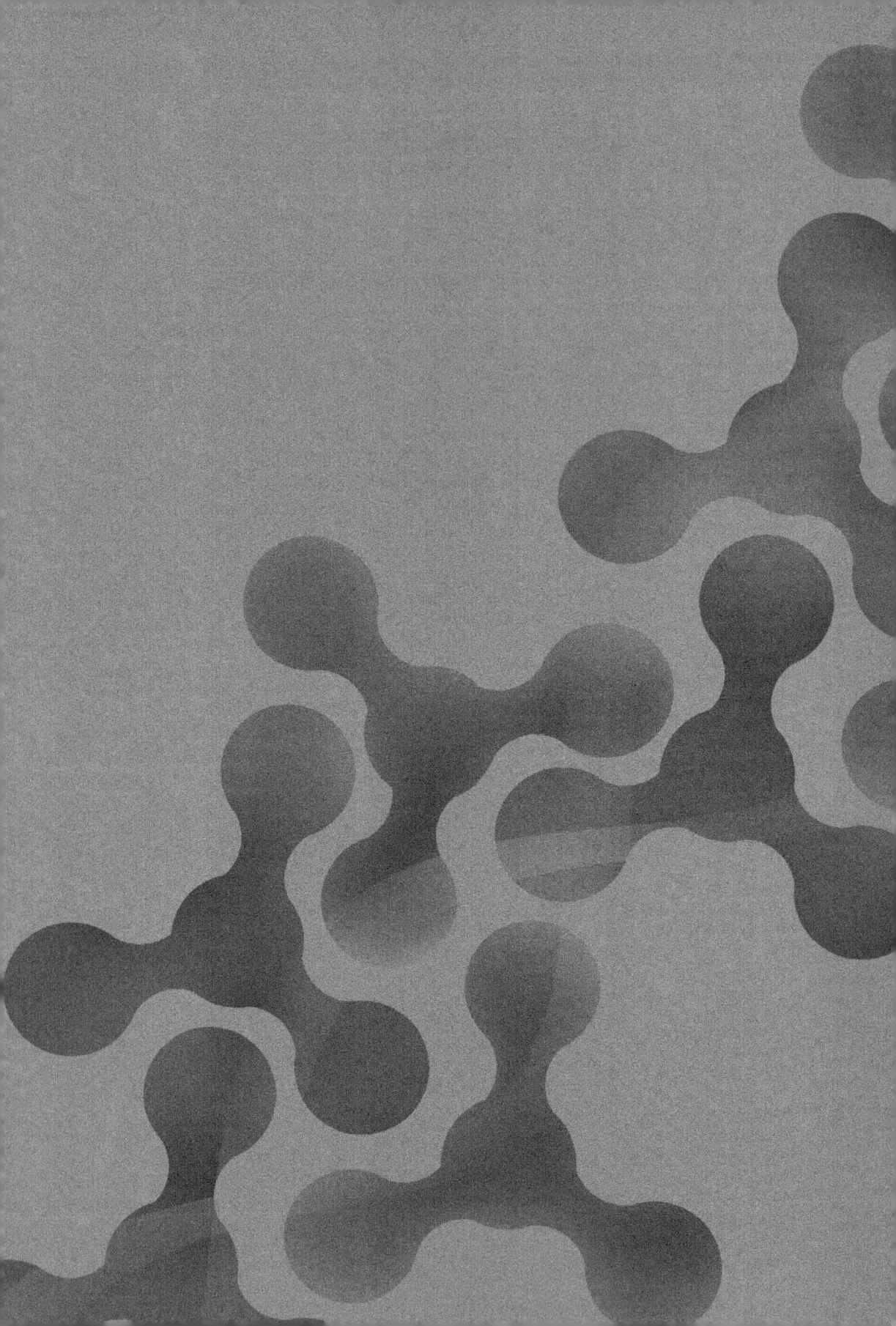

6. Assessment of project excellence

6.1. Purposes and approaches to the project excellence assessment

Building excellence in project management drives performance in every organisation. Excellence enhances an organisation's ability to implement the organisation strategy and project objectives through a successful and consistent delivery. Companies that adhere to strong project management methods, including a detailed evaluation of scope and budget, ongoing risk management and measurement of project results, are consistently more successful than those who do not. Following a systematic project management approach gives projects and organisations a powerful competitive advantage and is a prerequisite for long-term success.

The assessment of project excellence is a thorough process that enables the project team to understand how to achieve success and to identify and use their strengths and improvement potential.

The new IPMA Project Excellence Baseline® (IPMA PEB) is an adaptable and open concept and is designed for various purposes:

- Driving continuous improvement within projects;
- Regular monitoring of the project's ability to deliver sustainable results on different levels (objectives, customer, project team, other stakeholders, environment);
- Assessment and continuous improvement of project management methods;
- Recognition of projects that proved to be excellent based on the IPMA Project Excellence Model (IPMA PEM) assessment;
- Recognition of projects striving for excellence;
- Supporting recognition of leadership and management performance;
- Complementing project audit tools;
- Complementing project management maturity assessment tools.

The IPMA PEM can be used as an assessment method for programmes as defined below and adapted for the purposes of the respective programme, taking into consideration its complexity.

Driving continuous improvement within projects

Every project requires continuous improvement in order to harness the response to change and create competitive advantage. Continuous improvement should not be considered as a standalone initiative or self-contained goal.

The IPMA PEM drives continuous improvement because it is a tool helping project teams to identify areas for improvement, to align the project objectives accordingly, to create skills and resources to launch and integrate improvements into a culture of strategic execution, to blend well-known practices as well as to implement continuously the Plan-Do-Check-Act (PDCA) principle.

Regular monitoring of a project's ability to deliver sustainable results

Regular monitoring of project development is essential for project success and sustainability.

Monitoring tracks progress against set plans, checks compliance with established standards, helps to identify trends and patterns, adapts strategies and supports the implementation of decisions. It is imperative to put in place a well-planned monitoring mechanism to assess the project status and ensure sustainable results. Every project regularly monitors a variety of information according to its specific needs (e.g. monitoring of results, processes, compliance, context, stakeholder involvement, financials, organisation, etc.).

The IPMA PEM checks whether monitoring is systematically applied, based upon predefined indicators and assumptions. Monitoring needs to be timely and involves all key stakeholders in order to build understanding, ownership and accountability.

Assessment and continuous improvement of project management methods

Successful projects have well-established project management methods in place. Their active use, proper assessment and constant improvement are essential parts of project success.

The IPMA PEM helps to check the project management methods in use and assesses to what extent they are used within the project. The results of the IPMA PEM assessment can be useful for quality, knowledge and/or process managers to identify areas for improvement, to capture innovation and to collect lessons learnt in a structured way. The IPMA PEM also enables organisations to structure capitalisation of their project experience.

Recognition of projects that proved to be excellent based on the IPMA PEM assessment

IPMA rewards excellent projects through the IPMA Global Project Excellence Awards. The awards support professional project management in recognising high performance in projects. It motivates project teams to identify their strengths and optimise their use.

The intention of the IPMA Global Project Excellence Awards is to increase the recognition of projects from different countries, different industries and different organisations and to motivate project teams to develop and improve project management and to compare themselves against international benchmarks or set new ones. It supports professional project management in achieving high performance and identifies projects that exemplify excellent project management. By rewarding teams that prove their success in project management, IPMA recognises and acknowledges excellent and innovative projects.

The IPMA PEM helps a project team to reflect on its own strengths and potential improvement areas. It also helps the team understand the assessment process for the IPMA Global Project Excellence Award.

Project teams and organisations can assess themselves by using the model. They can find out in which areas their project work can be improved, and gain insight into what promising project management looks like. However, project teams can only learn from solid facts and findings. As a rule, subjective opinions provide little sound knowledge when determining project quality. To help assess any project, a fundamental and sound structure is required and this is provided by the IPMA PEM. Therefore, an external assessment by an IPMA Global Project Excellence Award assessment team offers a unique form of benchmarking for the project work. The Feedback Report gives the applicant's organisation crucial feedback that could lead to better project results in the future, provided that it functions as a 'learning organisation', able to take the necessary corrective actions for continuous improvement.

In some cases, the IPMA Global Project Excellence Award assessment results show that a project still has some way to go in order to achieve excellence. The main reason for this is that the assessed improvement potential in such projects is higher than that in other projects that have been recognised as excellent. The feedback for such a project, has an even higher relevance for the applicant's organisation, as they will be able to use the IPMA PEM to identify the areas where there is a gap against international benchmarks and so develop their project approach.

More information about the IPMA Global Project Excellence Award and the assessment process in particular can be found in Annex C.

Support recognition of leadership and management performance

IPMA ICB is a comprehensive and widely used model for assessing the competences of individuals in three domains: people, practice and perspective. It can be used for the certification of individuals, competence assessment and planning of professional development. In this context, the results of the IPMA PEM assessment of projects can be used to provide valuable, factual information about the actual performance of leaders in all three individual competence areas covered by the IPMA Individual Competence Baseline (IPMA ICB®).

Use of the model for project audit purposes

The IPMA PEM provides a framework that ensures the proper planning of project audit activities, while taking into consideration all the key areas influencing a projects' ability to succeed. The key benefits of using the model in this context are:
- Easy reporting on various levels;
- Inclusion of leadership as one of the key dimensions of management;
- Inherent link between observable processes and results.

When the IPMA PEM is used to support audit activities, it is recommended to supplement area B (Processes & Resources) with additional, detailed process requirements relevant to the nature of the project (construction, organisational change, software development etc.). Similarly, area A (People & Purpose) should be supported by relevant documents describing organisational values, culture and overall strategy, preferably supported by guidelines relevant to the portfolio that contains the audited project.

Whenever results of an audit based on the IPMA PEM framework are presented, it is recommended to highlight the connection of findings in areas A and B with project results and performance, observed as a result of area C assessment. This gives an important perspective on the actual effectiveness of these processes and their impact on stakeholders' satisfaction.

Use of the model for project management maturity assessments

The IPMA PEM is not designed as a maturity assessment tool, as it follows a different philosophy. Most maturity models focus on the existence, standardisation, optimisation and organisation-wide use of particular management techniques and practices that are expected by their authors. The IPMA PEM focuses on a conscious adaptability and continuous improvement in areas of project management that go beyond processes. It also closely links the assessment of methods with achieved results, which is not typical in most traditional maturity models.

6.2. Assessment of project excellence in a project lifecycle

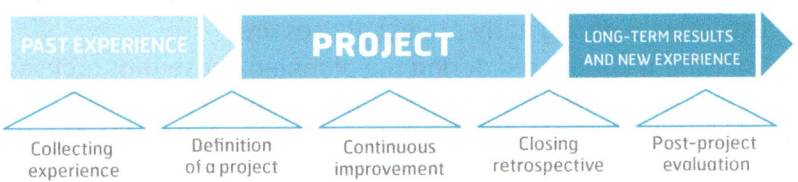

Figure 6-1: The use of IPMA PEM at various stages of the project lifecycle

Every project has certain phases of development. A clear understanding of these phases allows project leaders and executives to maintain control of the project more efficiently. The project lifecycle may differ, in both the number of phases it has and the detail within each of these phases. Collecting previous experiences, defining the project properly in its entirety (starting from business needs, benefits and objectives, including costs, resources, process definitions and continuous improvement) enable the successful delivery of the project.

Assessing a project during its different phases leads to a better understanding of the project context and the way it sets out to realise its objectives. The assessment can be used to help identify the most appropriate leadership style, management processes and resources for the achievement of project success. At later stages, when the first results are visible, these can also be taken into account to see how the approach selected leads to performance. Assessing a project helps to identify areas that are going well, as well as areas for improvement that the project leaders need to address. It turns the IPMA PEB into a powerful tool to help leaders achieve their objectives.

The project excellence assessment can be conducted focusing on the defined assessment criteria for project management, allowing strengths and improvement areas to be identified quickly. However, a full project excellence assessment also requires that results are assessed. This is normally possible only towards the end or after the delivery of the project.

How to use the IPMA PEM in the early project phases/midway through the project

The project excellence assessment can be conducted during the early project phases or midway through the project. In this case, the focus will be on the People & Purpose and Process & Resources criteria. Results cannot be fully assessed at this stage. Only certain results will be ready for assessment and some trends may be derived. Nevertheless, an assessment before the end of the project is beneficial and recommended. This will give the project team feedback on the project while corrective actions are still possible, help the project members to align their approach for the upcoming phases and will make best use of the IPMA PEM 'striving for improvement' report and implementation of lessons learnt. Two typical forms of an assessment during early project phases are:

- An assessment conducted during the planning phase that focuses mainly on whether the project has been set up so that the key success factors of the IPMA PEM have been considered and implemented in the project setup;
- An assessment during implementation. This can be conducted at several points in time to ensure the project is on track and following the project plan.

How to use the IPMA PEM in late project phases/towards project closure

At this point, the assessment can be conducted in full, with a strong focus on the Results criteria of the model.

The assessment results help the project team to self-reflect on their own strengths and potential for improvement. It can also help the permanent organisation ensure that the assessment feedback is considered in projects that are still at earlier stages in their lifecycle.

Projects that apply for the IPMA Global Project Excellence Award are required to be sufficiently far in the project lifecycle so that a full assessment can be carried out.

In general, the IPMA PEM is an assessment that can be applied throughout the project lifecycle and serves as a strong backbone for implementing proven project success factors and identifying areas for further improvement. It also helps the project team to self-reflect and finally ensures a full project assessment (including assessment of results after completion), capturing lessons learnt for future projects.

6.3. Scope of the assessment in projects, programmes and portfolios

One of the key decisions to be made when starting a project excellence assessment is on the scope to be assessed. This decision is always made after considering the objectives of the particular assessment effort. In addition, the business context of the assessed project (e.g. organisational setup, cooperation model, links to other projects or programmes, position in the overall portfolio) should be carefully analysed and defined.

There are three typical scenarios in which an assessment can be carried out:
- Assessment of an individual project;
- Assessment of a programme;
- Assessment of a representative project that is part of a portfolio.

Assessment of an individual project

When assessing an individual project, the scope of the assessment typically covers the entire scope of the project. It is also advised to cover the entire project lifecycle up to the day when the assessment is conducted, which is usually some time after the final delivery of the project. This ensures that findings show the improvement trends and demonstrate the effectiveness of the management through analysis of all available results (partial and/or final). This is especially important when assessing projects that were initially managed badly and/or have had to recover from major crises.

When assessing an individual project, the assessors generally need to ask themselves:
- To what extent should the influence of the overall management processes and leadership within the permanent organisation be taken into account?
- How do we treat projects using mature, in-house management methodologies supported by effective tools provided by the permanent organisation, given that the project leaders are unable to influence these with respect to their project execution?
- How do we treat the cultural influence of the permanent organisation and/or the dominating culture in a given region where the project is conducted?

It is advised to answer these questions keeping the following principles in mind:
- The IPMA PEM is designed to assess an individual project and its leadership, not the permanent organisation (see the IPMA Organisational Competence Baseline (IPMA OCB®) and IPMA Delta® for that purpose).
- Whenever the maturity of the permanent organisation and quality of the leadership have a positive or negative impact on any of the model criteria, it should be reflected by the assessment results, e.g.:
  - If the permanent organisation provides a standardised and mature management model that is successfully implemented within the project and leads to success, it should receive a positive score in the relevant criteria (e.g. B.1., B.2.), just like any other project following an equally mature approach.
  - If an inadequate leadership style within the permanent organisation jeopardises project efforts (e.g. through the lack of proper sponsorship), the project should receive a lower score in the relevant criteria (e.g. A.1., A.2.).
- What matters most in an IPMA PEM assessment is the conscious application and use of a suitable management approach and leadership style. Therefore, assessors should always verify to what extent the approach offered by the permanent organisation was evaluated by the project leaders and consciously chosen for its fit with or adapted to the needs of the project.
- Whenever cultural norms in a given project context are in conflict with values (e.g. anti-corruption) promoted by the IPMA PEM, the context cannot be taken as an excuse for not following them. However, all efforts to live up to the values promoted within the IPMA PEM should be scored favourably in the assessed project.
- Breaking strong cultural norms in a local environment can be considered as innovation, especially when assessing the People & Purpose area.

Assessment of a programme

The programme is defined as a 'temporary organisation of interrelated programme components (constituent initiatives) managed in a coordinated way to enable the implementation of change and the realisation of benefits. In practice, it is a group of related projects managed in a coordinated way to obtain benefits and control, beyond what is possible from managing them individually. Many, if not most, mega-projects that will use the IPMA PEM are in fact programmes, and a proper understanding of the actual scope for the assessment is crucial in order to be clear on where the assessment efforts should be focused, as well as to understand the validity of the assessment results.

There are three general approaches to assessing a programme using the IPMA PEM (see Figures):
- Assessment of the overall programme management;
- Assessment of the individual project within a programme;
- Assessment of the entire programme, including sub-programmes and individual projects.

Assessment of overall programme management

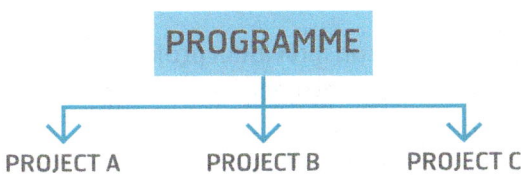

Figure 6-2: Scope of the overall programme management assessment

The primary goal of a programme assessment as described before is to provide feedback on the level of excellence of the overall programme management. It is a very efficient way to assess the overall condition of the programme without the need to conduct a number of assessments of individual projects.

In this case, the scope of the assessment of areas A and B of the model typically includes:
- Overall management of the programme strategy, objectives and scope;
- Key stakeholder management from the perspective of the programme management team;
- Leadership at the level of the programme management team;
- Processes to manage the programme as a whole and coordination of activities between projects.

Results are assessed from the overall programme business case perspective.

Whenever the project team is mentioned in the assessment criteria (e.g. in A.3.), the primary focus of the assessors should be on:
- The programme management team;
- The programme management/support office staff;
- The sub-programme(s) and project managers.

Assessment of an individual project within a programme

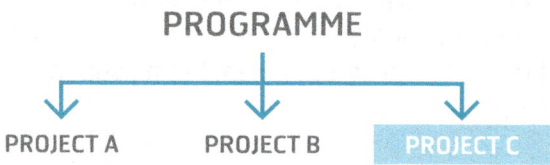

Figure 6-3: Scope of the individual project assessment within a programme

Principles for the assessment of an individual project within a programme do not differ from assessing a standalone project that is not part of a programme (see Assessment of an individual project).

However, in this case, assessment teams can experience difficulties related to interactions within the programme. It is therefore essential to start this type of assessment with a detailed analysis of the overall programme structure and the interactions between its components. This should be followed by a very precise definition of the scope of the assessment. Processes provided by the programme should only be taken into consideration when they directly impact the management of the individual project being assessed.

Assessment of the entire programme, including sub-programmes and individual projects

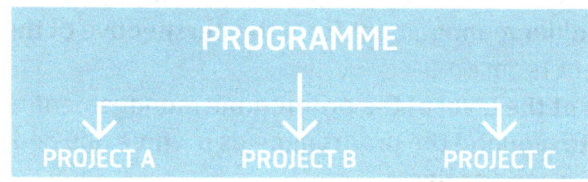

Figure 6-4: Scope of assessment of an entire programme

Whenever there is a need to obtain a complete and detailed picture of the management excellence of a programme, it is advised to include both the overall programme management and the management of individual projects in the scope of the assessment.

This is the most complex assessment task and should always be organised with special attention to planning and resources.

There are three possible approaches to such a complex assessment:
- **Assessment of the entire programme.** Here, the programme is assessed as a complex project, without dividing it into sub-components. Each of the projects or sub-projects is treated as a work package within a project.
- **Assessment of the overall programme management level, combined with assessments of all the individual projects.** This approach combines the two approaches described in previous sections (Assessment of the individual project within a programme and Assessment of overall programme management). Findings from these assessments are then combined to provide a complete picture of the level of excellence of the programme.
- **Assessment of the overall programme management level, combined with assessments of a sample of individual projects.** This approach is similar to the one described above. It requires less effort while still providing quality findings on all programme levels. The sample of projects should be carefully chosen in order to obtain objective results. This approach is used within an IPMA Delta assessment combining the self-assessment of a number of sample projects (P module) with an overall external assessment of the programme management (and, if applicable, portfolio management) at organisational level (O module).

Assessment of representative projects in a portfolio

Because the management of portfolios differs significantly from that of projects and programmes, the IPMA PEB cannot be applied directly to assess the excellence of portfolio management.

However, the model can be used to assess a sample of projects within a portfolio (see reference to the IPMA Delta assessment above). In this way, portfolio managers can obtain valuable feedback on the excellence of leadership and processes within these projects and observe their impact on project results. This can lead to improvement suggestions for management processes and leadership at the portfolio and individual project management level.

6.4. The role and competences of project excellence assessors

The assessors are the heart of the assessment process. Their key responsibilities are to set up the process and to carry out an objective assessment based on the IPMA PEM criteria.

Characteristics of a project excellence assessor:
- Strong project/programme management competences and experience in the practice domain:
    - Is an acting professional in the project/programme management field, preferably possessing an IPMA certification or similar;
    - Has experience in working as a project manager and/or as a project management consultant and/or as a quality expert.

- Strong competences in people and perspective domains:
    - Is a team player when working in an assessment team;
    - Is flexible and open to new approaches, methods, procedures and tools;
    - Is able understand the context of the project and its complexity;
    - Appreciates and understands cultural diversity;
    - Is reliable and diligent in carrying out all duties in the assessment process from start to finish;
    - Adheres to the principles of confidentiality and the IPMA Code of Ethics and Professional Conduct [7];
    - Adheres to the Assessors IPMA Code of Conduct.

- Actively developed IPMA PEM expertise:
    - Has participated in regular IPMA PEM training and is an active participant in the project excellence assessor community;
    - Has experience in using the IPMA PEM for project assessments;
    - Is able to write a Feedback Report with the assessment results describing strengths and areas for improvement based on the IPMA PEM criteria;
    - Acts as a good ambassador of project excellence, promoting the IPMA PEM based on the IPMA PEB.

The assessors for the assessment of projects within organisations can be chosen among experienced project managers, quality experts and PMO/PfMO staff members. Participation in an IPMA PEM assessment will help to capitalise on their experience and will further develop their competences through observation and analysis of various project situations within assessed projects. It can also strengthen constructive dialogue between these groups of professionals, leading to joint improvement of management methods.

The assessors that participate in the IPMA Global Project Excellence Award assessments are selected and allocated to a project by the Awards Coordinator, IPMA Vice President and Awards PMO.

6.5. The assessment process

This section describes a standard process of assessment that can be carried out by any organisation, either internally (self-assessment) or as an external service. For more details on the assessment process used by the IPMA Global Project Excellence Award, please refer to Annex C.

The assessment process can be conducted by an individual assessor or a team of assessors. These assessors should not be members of the assessed project team. This helps ensure that results are objective and gives the opportunity to use the assessment as a knowledge-sharing exercise.

If there is more than one assessor, a Team Lead Assessor (TLA) should be appointed. His or her role is to assure a proper assessment process and to coordinate delivery of the assessment results in a Feedback Report. If the assessment is being performed by a single assessor, he or she must also perform the TLA duties as described below.

Before the assessment, the TLA (often together with the assessment team) and project manager (or other relevant contact persons on behalf of the project) should agree on the following aspects of the assessment:
- Purpose (see paragraph 6.1.);
- Objectives (e.g. expected results);
- Scope (see paragraph 6.3.);
- Process (e.g. people involved, timelines, form of the report).

They should also clarify upfront any documents they need in order to prepare for the assessment process (they can provide a list of the documents they require before the start of the assessment). All documents should be available for verification on site during the assessment.

The TLA should ensure proper planning and coordination of all the assessors' activities ahead of and during the assessment. That includes the creation of interview plans.

From an individual assessor's perspective (either as part of a team or conducting an individual assessment) the following steps have to be followed:
1. Familiarisation with the initial set of project documents, such as project charter, project management plan, baselines, performance reports, satisfaction surveys, closure report (if available);
2. Initial IPMA PEM assessment based on documentation;
3. Together with the other assessors, reaching a common understanding of the initial assessment;
4. Creating a list of questions to ask during the interviews and a list of documents to review;

5. Conducting interviews with key project stakeholders, reviewing project documents to address remaining questions based on the IPMA PEM and confirming earlier findings based on documentation;
6. Together with the other assessors, reaching consensus on the final assessment.

The assessment results are then documented in a Feedback Report and presented to the project manager and interested parties. The report should cover the assessed IPMA PEM criteria, with assessment information about strengths and potential for improvements where found.

During the assessment, different techniques are used:
- Interviews;
- Document analysis;
- Demonstration (e.g. of the tools);
- site visit;
- Observation.

The IPMA PEM refers to qualitative and quantitative performance indicators that can be used during the assessment process:
- **Qualitative data** deal with descriptions and can, for example, be generated through interviews. Qualitative data can be observed, but not measured. Descriptions of experience or situations, or observations of behaviour are examples of qualitative data.
- **Quantitative data** deal with numbers and data, which can be objectively measured.

Length, height, area, volume, weight, speed, time, temperature, humidity, sound levels, cost, members, ages, KPIs etc. are examples of quantitative data.

6.6. Scoring approach

Whenever the IPMA PEM is used for continuous improvement and/or benchmarking purposes, a scoring system is recommended to assess against the model criteria. The overall approach to scoring is described below, while detailed scoring tables can be found in Annex B.

Scoring the People & Purpose and Processes & Resources criteria

Assessment of the People & Purpose and Processes & Resources criteria uses an approach based on the PDCA cycle. Findings in each of these criteria are scored individually on sub-criteria level (e.g. A.1a.) using a four-column table (see Figure 6-5).

PLAN	DO	CHECK	ACT
Defining a sound approach	Applying an approach systematically	Monitoring and analysing results of chosen approach	Improving and integrating the approach

Figure 6-5: Criteria for scoring areas A and B

- **Plan (defining a sound approach).** How the project team selects the overall project strategy, procedures, methods, approaches and tools that are appropriate to plan, execute, monitor and control the project and reflect the complexity of the project. Sources considered by the team may include industry and/or company management standards and methodologies, specific definitions of processes or process elements created for the project, etc.
- **Do (applying an approach systematically).** How the project team implemented the selected approach in the actual project. This column also verifies whether sufficient resources (human, technical, material) have been allocated for the successful execution of the planned approach.

- **Check (monitoring and analysing results of the chosen approach).** This column assesses two dimensions:
  - **Project management.** How the project team regularly checks whether the processes and tools used in the project are (still) appropriate and optimal for it and will lead to expected results;
  - **Project results.** How the project team regularly checks whether the progress of the project and achieved partial or final results are according to the planned approach.
- **Act (improving and integrating the approach).** This column is used to score the way the project team reacts to findings from the regular monitoring and results analysis. As with the previous column, this column addresses two dimensions;
  - **Project management.** How the project team drives changes to procedures, methods, approaches and tools, in order to ensure they are optimally appropriate for planning, executing, monitoring and controlling the project.
  - **Project results.** How the project team develops and implements actions to bring the project back on track.

Scoring the various stakeholders' satisfaction levels

The assessment of the various stakeholders' satisfaction levels focuses on two dimensions:
- The stakeholders' own perception;
- Independent indicators.

Both dimensions are linked to the management approach and compared with an industry benchmark using a four-column scoring table on criteria level (e.g. C.1.):

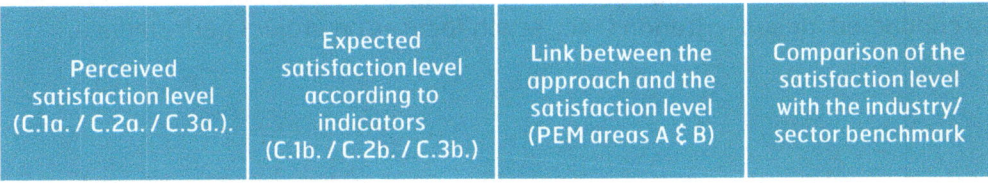

Figure 6-6: Criteria for scoring stakeholder satisfaction

- **Perceived satisfaction level.** How a given group of stakeholders (e.g. customer representatives in criterion C.1.) judge their satisfaction themselves. This column takes into account only the direct statements of stakeholders, obtained, for example, by interviewing them, or by project satisfaction surveys, recommendation letters, press releases etc.
- **Expected satisfaction level according to indicators.** The satisfaction level that can be expected based on observing independent indicators, e.g. meeting acceptance criteria, amount and nature of claims, growth of the stakeholders' business as a result of the project etc.
- **Link between the approach and satisfaction level.** The extent to which the approach to managing the project has contributed to the observed satisfaction level. This column provides a key link to the People & Purpose and Processes & Resources criteria and, as such, should have a significant impact on overall score for a given criterion.
- **Comparison of the satisfaction level with the industry/sector benchmark.** How the actual satisfaction level of given stakeholders, also considering independent indicators, compares against the industry or sector benchmark. This column helps to calibrate the observed satisfaction level with what is usually expected in this kind of project within a given industry or sector. Even though satisfaction might not always be high (e.g. when lay-offs are part of the project), it might still be exceptional when compared with similar projects.

Scoring the project results

The assessment of the project results focuses on two dimensions:
- Results of the project as defined in project objectives and beyond (sub-criteria C.4a. and C.4b.);
- Project performance (sub-criterion C.4c.).

Sub-criteria C.4a. and C.4b. should be scored together as both relate to various project results, including impact on the environment. Separate scoring should be conducted for sub-criterion C.4c., which focuses on project performance.

Results and performance are assessed using a four-column scoring table (see Figure 6-7):

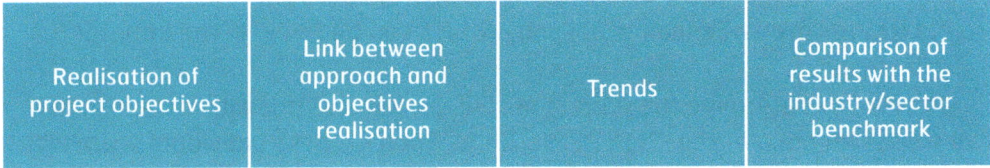

Figure 6-7: Criteria for scoring project results

- **Realisation of project objectives**. This column is used in order to compare project results and performance with objectives set within the project. Whenever this column is used for assessing results (criteria C.4a. and C.4b.), it is essential to take findings from both of these criteria into account. It is expected that excellent projects have a mostly positive impact on their environment and deliver results well beyond expectations.
- **Link between the approach and objectives realisation**. This column is about the extent to which the approach to managing the project has contributed to the results and performance achieved. It provides a link to both the People & Purpose and Processes & Resources criteria and, as such, should have a significant impact on overall score for a given criterion.
- **Trends**. The purpose of this column is to assess whether the project achieved its results and performance consistently across all its phases. Good examples might include consistently on-time delivery, meeting quality requirements for all key deliverables or a consistently low number of incidents.
- **Comparison of results with the industry/sector benchmark**. This column helps to calibrate the observed results and performance level with those usually expected in this kind of project in a given industry or sector. The expectation is that in an excellent project the leaders are aware of industry and sector benchmark projects and the relative position of their own project when compared with them.

Determining the project profile

The final outcome of the scoring process is a project profile that consists of three general scores, respectively for People & Purpose, Processes & Resources and Project Results areas. Examples of such profiles can be found in the Chapter 5.3 of this baseline.

In order to determine the project profile, assessors start with sixteen individual scores for each of the IPMA PEM criteria. Each of these individual scores is determined using a relevant scoring table as described earlier in this chapter.

The final score for each of the IPMA PEM areas is then calculated using the following formulas:
- **People & Purpose:**
  ((A.1a. + A.1b. + A.1c.) / 3 + (A.2a. + A.2b. + A.2c.) / 3 + (A.3a. + A.3b. + A.3c.) / 3) / 3
- **Processes & Resources:**
  (B.1. + B.2.) / 2
- **Project Results:**
  ((C.1. + C.2. + C.3.) / 3 + (C.4ab. + C.4c.) / 2) / 2

Annex A:
Description of the Project Excellence Model

A. People & Purpose

The People & Purpose area follows the logic that project excellence starts with leaders, including sponsors, who define and follow the right values and consciously apply an effective leadership style. These leaders engage key stakeholders in the definition of the project objectives and strategy formulation. They build effective teams and engage the right partners and suppliers in order to achieve project success.

A.1. Leadership & Values

Excellent projects are led in a way that anticipates the future and realises it with persistence. The leaders (i.e. all the people involved in a leadership/managerial role within the project or from the client/line organisation) act as role models for the project team with respect to values, morals, focus on objectives, working standards, self-management and cooperation, and create a high-trust, high-inspiration environment. Leaders enable and authorise the project team to anticipate and act in time to achieve project success. They support a flexible project organisation capable of adapting to changing circumstances.

A.1a. Role models for excellence

Leaders communicate and live up to their values (i.e. they 'walk the talk'), follow ethical standards and act as role models. They ensure that structures and norms are in place that enable project team members to work effectively and efficiently. Leaders build and strengthen a culture of excellence and continuous improvement both within and beyond the project. They observe and carry out the project excellence concepts in a credible way and stimulate others to do the same.

In practice, leaders of excellent projects:
- Are role models for integrity, social responsibility, ethical behaviour (e.g. as defined in the UN Global Compact's Ten Principles in the areas of human rights, labour, the environment and anti-corruption) and the project excellence philosophy, both within the project and its environment (e.g. towards the line organisation, clients, partners, suppliers etc.) and ensure the project team members adopt and live up to these values;
- Promote the organisation's values in the project;
- Understand the concept of continuous improvement and champion its application in the project and beyond;
- Actively seek feedback from different stakeholders to improve their leadership approach;

- Regularly take time to reflect on their own role, behaviour and impact;
- Review and improve the effectiveness of leadership behaviour including their own;
- Strive for personal excellence by reviewing and improving their own competences;
- Inspire project team members to strive for excellence in their behaviour and working methods, keeping in mind the objectives of the project;
- Systematically integrate project team members into the continuous improvement process;
- Foster innovation in the project and encourage project team members to do the same.

A.1b. Care for project stakeholders

Leaders care for internal and external stakeholders. They are proactively engaged in balancing the needs and interests of different parties, supporting their development and striving to provide a good working environment. They ensure that the impact of the project on its environment is recognised and actively managed to ensure sustainability.

In practice, leaders of excellent projects:
- Behave in a socially responsible way, taking a balanced approach to all stakeholders' interests (including the interests of stakeholders with limited power);
- Personally engage in a dialogue with stakeholders;
- Ensure that management structures create the space and capacity for maintaining relations with key stakeholders;
- Understand the key elements of the project environment, including its natural environment, social systems and economy;
- Whenever applicable, recognise environmental bodies and organisations as project stakeholders, address their needs in balance with the project objectives and cooperate with them if and when needed;
- Create a safety-conscious environment for team members and other relevant stakeholders, also extending to clients, partners and suppliers;
- Create and promote dialogue among stakeholders that leads to mutual care and a good working atmosphere;
- Consider the impact of their decisions on the project team, partners and suppliers, e.g. their health, work/life balance etc.;
- Meet regulatory requirements, guidelines and/or standards geared towards caring for relevant stakeholders and the environment;
- Promote activities that lead to stakeholders' development and growth.

A.1c. Orientation towards project objectives and adaptability to change

Project leaders take responsibility for short- and long-term project results (i.e. benefits), ensuring successful project delivery. They ensure sustainability of project results including, if applicable, the consequences for future generations. They listen to stakeholders, observe the project environment and create space for dialogue about different approaches and innovation.

In practice, leaders of excellent projects:
- Ensure a constant focus on short- and long-term objectives;
- Set and communicate a clear, long-term vision that goes beyond the moment of project completion (i.e. delivery of the objectives);
- Review, adapt and realign the project strategy when necessary, inspiring trust at all times;
- Unite team members and all other relevant stakeholders in sharing and achieving the project vision, objectives and values;
- Create an environment where team members and all other relevant stakeholders (e.g. partners and suppliers) take responsibility for the project objectives and results as a whole;
- Actively strive to remove obstacles that block or limit team members, partners and suppliers from successfully fulfilling their responsibilities;
- Create a flexible project organisation able to respond (e.g. adapt ways of working) to a changing environment;
- Actively involve stakeholders relevant for the realisation and sustainability of the long-term project results;
- Establish approaches that enable partners, customers and other relevant stakeholders to generate ideas and innovations and engage them in doing so;
- Promote a culture that supports the generation and development of new ideas and new ways of thinking to encourage innovation and organisational development.

A.2. Objectives & Strategy

The objectives and strategies of excellent projects are defined and developed by the project leaders in alignment with stakeholders' needs and requirements. They also take into account the project environment. Once agreed, objectives and strategies are regularly reviewed and, if necessary, adapted in response to a changing environment or to stakeholder demands. Excellent projects use project objectives and overall project strategies to develop and continuously adapt their plans and procedures.

A.2a. Managing stakeholders' needs, expectations and requirements

Stakeholders, their needs, expectations and requirements are clearly identified and actively managed.

In practice, excellent projects:
- Systematically identify all relevant and potential stakeholders, including relationships between them;
- Understand the potential positive and negative impact of stakeholders on the ability of the project to reach its objectives;
- Regularly check whether additional stakeholders need to be considered;
- Observe changes in the stakeholder landscape and react to them;
- Actively pursue interaction with stakeholders and ensure that they are involved when appropriate;
- Define and implement effective processes for the engagement of stakeholders, taking into account organisational and social complexity;
- Develop and regularly apply approaches to understanding, anticipating and responding to their different needs, expectations and requirements;
- Identify and record the needs, expectations and requirements of various stakeholders;
- Identify values and/or objectives important to stakeholders (e.g. safety, environment protection, sustainability, quality, time to market) in order to incorporate them in the development of project objectives and strategy;
- Actively seek common goals and values and use them to create project allies of stakeholders whenever possible;
- Recognise changes in stakeholder needs, expectations and requirements;
- Proactively and transparently communicate the decisions related to stakeholders' requirements and their fulfilment;

- Systematically compare the project results with the expectations and requirements of stakeholders in order to monitor the effectiveness of the approach or the solution chosen to satisfy them;
- Actively integrate stakeholders in the process of continuous learning throughout the project lifecycle.

A.2b. Development and realisation of project objectives

Project objectives are developed from a comprehensive analysis of relevant information. Competing interests are dealt with. Stakeholders are familiar with the relevant objectives and understand their role in achieving them. Objectives are regularly reviewed, and adapted to changes in stakeholders' expectations and requirements when necessary.

In practice, excellent projects:
- Seek relevant sources of information for developing project objectives (e.g. contractual requirements, corporate strategy and business model, stakeholders, standards, market conditions, legal etc.) and ensure a proper prioritisation of these sources;
- Whenever possible, actively involve relevant stakeholders in formulating project objectives;
- Use information from stakeholder analyses when developing project objectives, also considering the project environment;
- Look for possibilities for aligning the objectives of stakeholders (e.g. suppliers, team members, partners) with the objectives of the project to ensure their buy-in and maximise their contribution;
- Recognise competing and/or conflicting interests and find appropriate solutions (e.g. integration, rejection, looking for alternatives);
- Use a consensus approach to deal with conflicting interests;
- Benchmark with similar projects and use conclusions where relevant for the development of the project objectives;
- Ensure that the objectives clearly address sustainability, environment, security, health and safety requirements adequate to the type of project;
- Ensure compliance of the objectives with legal and regulatory requirements;
- Recognise the impact that achieving project objectives (e.g. a reduction of the workforce) would have on stakeholders and the project environment and use this knowledge for the further development of project objectives and/or strategy;
- Verify whether objectives are specific, measurable, achievable, relevant and time bound;
- Secure the commitment of the project team members to the project objectives;

- Inform stakeholders about relevant project objectives;
- Ensure that stakeholders understand relevant project objectives;
- Ensure that stakeholders who need to approve the project objectives commit to achieving them;
- Systematically adapt the project objectives in accordance with the changing needs, expectations and requirements of relevant stakeholders;
- Recognise and identify key factors and conditions for success;
- Use a balanced set of performance indicators and related outcomes to determine successful execution;
- Regularly check during the project lifecycle whether objectives can be reached and, if appropriate, take action (e.g. change approach, modify objectives, add or change resources).

A.2c. Development and realisation of project strategy

In excellent projects, project teams develop and implement an overall project strategy based on an evaluation of the project objectives, context and environment (including its position in the programme and/or project portfolio). The project strategy, together with the project objectives, enables the project team to focus on what is most important for the project to be successful.

In practice, excellent projects:
- Consider a range of external and internal factors (e.g. contractual requirements, corporate strategy and business models, stakeholders, standards, market conditions, legal etc.) when developing the project strategy;
- Identify key project values (e.g. safety, environment protection, sustainability, quality, time to market) and ensure that the project strategy is aligned with them;
- Decide on the most appropriate overall project management strategy (e.g. hub and spoke or centralised, traditional or agile, centralised or distributed, make or buy, lab or industrial) and business model for the project (e.g. financing and taxation models, overall distribution of benefits and risks, partnerships and contractual models) on the basis of a conscious evaluation;
- Ensure that the project's own strategy is aligned with the strategy and business model of the permanent organisation;
- Ensure that the project strategy addresses the needs, expectations and requirements of project stakeholders;
- Ensure that the project strategy is relevant to the organisational, social, political, legal and technical complexity of the project and its environment;
- Actively seek and evaluate innovations and learning opportunities and adapt the project strategy accordingly;

- Ensure that the project strategy includes the project governance approach (e.g. continuous alignment with organisation's strategy, supervision of business case, overall supervision model);
- Develop strategies for business continuity during the entire project lifecycle (e.g. overall risk management, emergency/disaster recovery plans, delegation/substitution matrices etc.);
- Ensure that project strategy takes care of transferring project results to appropriate stakeholders so that they are maintained in a sustainable way;
- Are aware of their own organisation's key competences, capabilities and abilities in order to work out strategies for forming partnerships that add value to the project;
- Align the project strategy to potential partners' strategies to create win-win situations and maximise their potential partners' commitment;
- Ensure the project team participates in developing the project strategy and obtains their commitment to it;
- Systematically monitor and analyse the project performance indicators in order to adapt the project strategy accordingly.

A.3. Project Team, Partners & Suppliers

In excellent projects, project team members, partners and suppliers are valued through the creation of a culture that allows the mutually beneficial achievement of organisational, project and personal goals. Fairness and equality are promoted within the project, with respect to integration and development of all involved parties.

In excellent projects, achievements are communicated, rewarded and recognised in a way that motivates project team members, partners and suppliers. This builds commitment and enables skills and knowledge to be used and developed in order to achieve project success.

A.3a. Identification and development of competences

Leaders recognise the competences required for project success in all three domains: people, practice and perspective [1]. They are aware of the capabilities, limitations and potential of their own organisation and those of their partners and suppliers. The organisations' own staff and third parties are taken into account when developing the project setup. Their competences are developed as required and when needed.

In practice, excellent projects:
- Identify the competences required for project success in all three domains: people, practice and perspective [1];
- Recognise the competences, capabilities and potential of project team members from their own organisation, partner(s) and supplier(s) organisations;
- Develop adequate staffing strategies and processes;
- Consider relevant policies (e.g. human resources (HR), code of conduct) and elements of the organisations' competence development culture and adapt them whenever necessary;
- Ensure transparency and fairness in project staffing processes;
- Promote and encourage equal opportunities and diversity;
- Manage staffing, development and release of project team members, together with the relevant staff (e.g. line managers, HR, project management office (PMO), procurement) from their own organisation, as well as partners and suppliers;
- Have a system in place for the managed and controlled release of people who can no longer contribute to achieving the project goals;
- Seek opportunities for team members to develop their personal competences while balancing personal, project and organisation objectives (e.g. employability, career path, fitness for organisational changes);
- Seek opportunities to contribute to the development of their organisation, its partners and suppliers;

- Carry out adequate competence development activities, also involving partners and suppliers when necessary;
- Check the effectiveness of the competence development activities and adapt the processes in place when needed;
- Take into account learning opportunities beyond training (e.g. by evaluations, analysis of mistakes, mentoring etc.).

A.3b. Recognition of achievements and empowerment

People are rewarded, recognised and taken care of by leaders. Project team members, partners and suppliers are enabled to realise their full potential when realising project objectives. They are involved in the ongoing processes and are empowered to take appropriate actions.

In practice, excellent projects:
- Define areas of responsibility for project team members, partners and suppliers and give them a clear mandate to take independent action to achieve results;
- Ensure that team members, partners and suppliers have the necessary authorisation levels, access to the project infrastructure, resources and information to be able to maximise their contribution;
- Involve project team members, partners and suppliers in defining the project management strategy and selecting appropriate project management methods, tools and processes;
- Recognise individuals', team members', partners' and suppliers' achievements in a timely and appropriate manner;
- Ensure that recognition of achievements is shared with the permanent organisation;
- Develop an open culture that encourages team members, partners and suppliers to discuss mistakes and to ask for support when facing and solving problems;
- Encourage team members, partners and suppliers to have an open mind set and use creativity and innovation to respond to the challenges they face;
- Involve team members, partners and suppliers in continuous reviews, improvements and optimisation of the effectiveness of their processes;
- Encourage team members, partners and suppliers to promote the project values and act accordingly (e.g. in the areas of safety, quality, care for stakeholders) and take independent action when these are at risk;
- Encourage team members to voice their (personal) opinions and ensure that these are followed up;
- Build true (i.e. intrinsic) motivation reaching beyond financial incentives;
- Encourage people to participate in activities that contribute to the organisation and to society.

A.3c. Collaboration and communication

The project organisation and processes are designed in ways that enable project team members, partners and suppliers to communicate and cooperate efficiently both within the project and beyond.

In practice, excellent projects:
- Create a culture of mutual involvement, open communication, trust, cooperation, collaboration, ownership, empowerment, improvement and accountability at all levels, also encompassing partners and suppliers;
- Build high-performance, integrated teams together with partners and suppliers as a key success factor;
- Ensure equal treatment of all team members, partners and suppliers, especially when it comes to the realisation of project values (e.g. safety, fairness, work/life balance);
- Ensure a good understanding of the communication needs and expectations of team members, customers, partners and suppliers;
- Develop and implement communication plans for efficient and effective communication at all levels;
- Encourage all team members to proactively communicate problems when they arise, and contribute to solving them;
- Ensure that the information necessary for team members, partners and suppliers to collaborate effectively is available and easily accessible in a timely fashion;
- Enable and encourage sharing of information, knowledge and best practices;
- Achieve a constructive form of dialogue within the project team and with other stakeholders;
- Proactively manage conflicts (e.g. through coaching, mediation);
- Ensure that effective escalation rules and/or procedures are in place;
- Gather regular feedback from project team members, partners and suppliers;
- Whenever applicable, ensure a continuous dialogue with the permanent organisation to maximise mutual benefits (both within and outside the project).

B. Processes & Resources

The Processes & Resources area focuses on the management of key processes contributing to project success and the resources required to realise them successfully. Given the importance of the project management processes and related resources, they receive special attention in the model. The project team should carefully select, adapt and develop them in order for the project to reach its goals in an effective and efficient way. Their adequacy for the needs of the project and its complexity should also be actively managed throughout the entire project lifecycle. However, effective and efficient project management processes alone are not sufficient conditions for project success. This is the main reason that the IPMA Project Excellence Model (IPMA PEM) also considers how the project team identifies other processes and resources required for project success and the way the project fits into its environment (e.g. corporate, legal, natural).

B.1. Project Management Processes & Resources

Teams on excellent projects identify the key project management processes and related resources necessary for project success in cooperation with stakeholders. Key methods, tools and project management processes are selected, developed and optimised to achieve the project objectives in the most effective and efficient way. This is done based on a good understanding of the project needs and organisational capabilities.

In practice, teams on excellent projects:
- Involve their stakeholders in the identification, alignment, implementation, evaluation and improvement of key project management processes;
- Define project management processes on the basis of good practices and lessons learnt from other projects, stakeholders and recognised industry/sector standards;
- Identify and implement appropriate project management processes, tools, methodologies, structures and resources for managing [4]:
    - integration
    - stakeholders
    - scope
    - resources
    - time
    - cost
    - risk
    - quality
    - procurement
    - communication

- When suitable to the project and/or sector context, identify and implement additional project management processes, tools, methodologies, structures and resources for managing areas such as:
  - safety
  - social responsibility
  - environmental protection
  - sustainability
  - security
  - knowledge and intellectual property
- Ensure that project management processes are adequate for the organisational, social, political, legal and technical complexity of the project and its environment;
- Manage, evaluate and improve project management processes and resources on a regular basis during the entire project lifecycle;
- Transfer the results of reviews back to the project, the organisation and other relevant stakeholders. Whenever possible, the project contributes to the development of the organisational competences of the performing organisation, its partners and customer;
- Align project management processes with corporate and project governance;
- Adhere to applicable rules and regulations (e.g. national/international standards and laws);
- Apply innovative project management approaches and value-adding improvements when appropriate;
- Introduce necessary project processes and procedures to relevant stakeholders and train them when needed;
- Formulate and monitor measurable process performance indicators and outcomes, clearly linked to the project objectives and results;
- Strive to improve industry or sector standards whenever possible;
- Monitor the effectiveness and efficiency of their project management processes and resources, such as by observing:
  - variations/scope changes
  - claims and resolutions
  - planned vs. actual budget (including financial resources, costs, risks, contingency)
  - cost of poor quality, deviation or non-conformance
  - planned vs. actual project progress (e.g. milestones and deliverables)
  - product quality: internal and external product inspection and audit recommendations and follow-up, repair, rework, scrap rates
  - process quality: internal and external process audit recommendations and follow-up

- safety related indicators (e.g. lost time incidents, (near) fatal accidents)
- internal and external issues and conflicts (e.g. resource conflicts, interpersonal issues).

B.2. Management of Other Key Processes & Resources

Teams on excellent projects identify other key project delivery and support processes and related resources necessary for project success (e.g. product design, engineering, maintenance, handover and acceptance, logistics, safety and security) in cooperation with stakeholders. These methods, tools and processes are selected, developed and optimised to achieve the project objectives in the most effective and efficient way. This is achieved based on a good understanding of organisational capabilities.

In practice, teams on excellent projects:
- Involve their stakeholders in identifying and executing key delivery and support processes in addition to the project management processes that are necessary for project success;
- Define their delivery and support processes on the basis of good practice and lessons learnt from other projects and recognised industry/sector standards;
- Prioritise the efforts (time and money) on the delivery and support processes based on the impact they have on the project success;
- Identify and implement appropriate project delivery, acceptance and support processes, tools, methodologies, structures and resources (existing or adapted) for managing areas such as:
  - product development and design
  - new technologies/R&D
  - engineering
  - compliance
  - commissioning and testing
  - (legal) approvals and/or permits
  - supply chain and logistics
  - assets (e.g. buildings, equipment and materials)
  - the environment (e.g. waste, CO_2 output, re-use of materials, recycling)
  - safety and security (e.g. worker, site, product)
  - product lifecycle
  - social impact (e.g. human rights, diversity and inclusion, effects of the project on the community)
  - handover/transition, including training and (gradual) acceptance
  - support processes such as: finance, accounting and HR support
- Monitor the effectiveness and efficiency of their project delivery and support processes and resources, such as by observing:
  - system performance and acceptance
  - waste reduction (e.g. materials, resources)
  - pollution levels

- use of raw vs. recycled materials
- use of non-renewable materials
- use of hazardous materials
- safety levels (e.g. lost time incidents, (near) fatal accidents, worker and public health and safety)
- security breaches
- timely permissions/permits
- number of revisions, including approvals and rejections (e.g. drawings)
- on-time delivery of goods and materials
- closed loop recycling management
- project image (e.g. awards won, recognition received in the media, publications and articles)
- Transfer the results of reviews back to the project, organisation and other relevant stakeholders;
- Whenever possible, ensure that the project contributes to the development of the competences of the organisation, its partners and customer(s);
- Adhere to applicable rules and regulations (e.g. national/international standards);
- Recognise the necessity of protecting various stakeholders' information assets and establish appropriate authorisation levels for information access on a 'need to know' basis;
- Apply innovative approaches and value-adding improvements when appropriate;
- Introduce the processes and procedures to relevant stakeholders and train them when needed;
- Formulate and monitor measurable process performance indicators and outcomes, clearly linked to the project objectives and results;
- Strive to improve industry and sector standards whenever possible.

C. Project Results

The Project Results area consists of criteria that provide insight into the perceptions about the management of the project held by the customer, project team members and other stakeholders, expressed in terms of their satisfaction levels, as well as indicators that prove these satisfaction levels. In addition, it covers other results that can provide insight into the level of excellence achieved by the project.

Balancing the expectations and demands of all parties involved, together with great management processes, should lead to sustainable and outstanding results for all key stakeholders. The concept of sustainability as an important element of project excellence is specifically explained in Chapter 4.4, 'The role of sustainability'. As a fundamental principle, results can, by definition, only be excellent if they are also sustainable, so fully evaluating the excellence of a project entails extrapolating from the results achieved at the end of a project, in order to estimate future levels of satisfaction and success.

C.1. Customer Satisfaction

Excellent projects achieve a high customer satisfaction. The perceived satisfaction is consistent with the fulfilment of the project objectives, key performance indicators (quantitative and qualitative), engagement of customer representatives and their identification with the project. In well-managed organisations and projects, the customer alone decides on the perception of quality. The customer satisfaction criterion is a reflection of how well the project team understood and fulfilled their needs and requirements.

C.1a. Customer perception
Customer representatives consistently express their satisfaction throughout the entire project lifecycle.

Useful examples might be:
- Written and/or verbal appreciation or recommendations expressed by various customer representatives;
- Satisfaction survey results and feedback from focus groups;
- Positive contribution to the long-term relationship with the customer is expressed;
- Formal appreciation and awards for project achievements are granted by the customer;

- Customer feedback that gives a clear statement about, for example:
  - fulfilment of needs and expectations
  - leadership and its accessibility
  - project management (e.g. planning, steering, change management, quality management, requirements, risk management, communication, lifecycle management, human resource management, deliverables and reporting)
  - cooperation between the project team and the customer
  - human aspects, project ethics, values and principles
  - project results
  - other benefits that originate from the project
  - achieved alignment to corporate/customer strategic goals
  - the customer's ability to realise their business case
  - long-term, sustainable results of the project
  - willingness to work on additional projects or tasks either within or beyond the contractual framework
  - recommendations to other business units or companies
  - positive lessons learnt and improvements to the customer's business.

C.1b. Indicators of customer satisfaction

In excellent projects, the perception expressed by customer representatives (C.1a.) and relevant observable indicators lead to the same conclusions about the customer satisfaction level.

Useful indicators might be:
- Benefits achieved as described in the business case;
- System performance and acceptance;
- Actual performance indicators related to the contract (e.g. budget, schedule or milestones, quality, deliverables, resources);
- The tone of the correspondence, i.e. positive (constructive) vs. negative (adverse);
- The degree of the acceptance (e.g. conditional vs. unconditional, number and nature of conditions in the sign-off protocol);
- Timeliness of response to change requests, claims and complaints;
- Number, nature and outcome of change requests;
- Number, nature and outcome of claims and resolutions;
- Number, nature and outcome of complaints and resolutions;
- Number, nature and amount of penalties and/or liquidated damages applied;
- Number of unresolved faults/defects (e.g. length and acceptability of the prioritisation of the punch list – i.e. the list of defects still to be remedied at the end of the contract);

- Number and nature of revisions of project related specifications (e.g. technical drawings);
- Number and nature of technical queries;
- Amount of non-conformance costs;
- Safety performance, e.g. lost time incidents, (near) fatal accidents, timely permissions/permits;
- Requests of the customer for new projects;
- Awards and formal appreciations received by the customer (e.g. product of the year, safest site of the year, recognition received in the media, publications and articles etc.);
- Changes to the contractors' valuation in the customer's vendor rating system;
- On-time delivery of goods and materials according to the plan.

C.2. Project Team Satisfaction

Excellent projects achieve high team member satisfaction. The perceived satisfaction is consistent with the fulfilment of the project objectives, engagement of the team members in the project and their identification with the team.

C.2a. Perception of the project team
Project team members consistently express their satisfaction throughout the entire project lifecycle.

Useful examples might be:
- Written or verbal appreciation and/or recommendations expressed by various team members, suppliers, partners, customers and/or other stakeholders;
- Feedback results of project team satisfaction statements/surveys;
- The project team satisfaction level could pertain to:
  - strategy and direction
  - confidence in the way the project is managed
  - senior leader behaviour, e.g. appreciation of the leadership
  - communication and collaboration in the team, with suppliers, partners and/or with other stakeholders
  - partnership and culture
  - respect and recognition
  - career development
  - cooperation between the project team and the customer
  - human aspects, project ethics, values and principles
  - fulfilment of (implicit and explicit) needs and expectations
  - performance management
  - trust, confidence and empowerment
  - work/life balance
  - corporate responsibility
  - personal and professional development.

C. 2b. Indicators of project team satisfaction
In excellent projects the perception expressed by team members (C.2a.) and relevant observable indicators lead to the same conclusions about the level of project team member satisfaction.

Useful indicators might be:
- Results of project team satisfaction surveys compared with planned results;
- Number of training days compared with planned number of days;

- Number/percentage of accepted and denied training requests;
- Sick level (number of sick days), especially with regard to 'burnouts';
- Safety performance, (e.g. lost time incidents, (near) fatal accidents);
- Turnover rate;
- Recognition and awards;
- Number of innovations and ideas for improvement proposed by team members;
- Number of complaints and their follow up;
- Recognition from senior management;
- Financial and/or non-financial rewards.

C.3. Other Stakeholder Satisfaction

Excellent projects achieve high stakeholder satisfaction. The perceived satisfaction is consistent with the fulfilment of the project objectives, key performance indicators (quantitative and qualitative), engagement of the stakeholders' representatives and their identification with the project. Stakeholders representing environmental aspects of the project are highly satisfied.

C.3a. Perception of the other stakeholders
Stakeholders consistently express their satisfaction throughout the entire project lifecycle. Positive impacts on the environment are measurable. Whenever the project has a considerable impact on the natural environment, the satisfaction of respective stakeholders (e.g. NGOs, local communities and/or authorities) is considered.

Useful examples might be:
- Written or verbal appreciation expressed by one or various stakeholders;
- Awards for project achievements granted by stakeholders;
- Positive results from stakeholder satisfaction surveys and feedback from focus groups;
- Positive results regarding the satisfaction of pro-environmental entities and environmentalists;
- Stakeholders' perceptions that give a clear perspective about, for example:
    - project management (e.g. planning, steering, change management, quality management, requirements, risk management, communication, lifecycle management, human resource management, deliverables and reporting)
    - adequate involvement of stakeholders in the project
    - long-term relationship
    - cooperation between the project team and the stakeholders
    - positive contribution to the environment
    - human aspects, project ethics, values and principles
    - direct and indirect project results
    - impact on nature (flora and fauna)
    - environmental impact, and consequences for society such as pollution (e.g. air, soil, water, noise, light), demographic change.

C.3b. Indicators of other stakeholders' satisfaction
In excellent projects the perception expressed by stakeholders (C.3a.) and relevant observable indicators lead to the same conclusions about the level of stakeholder satisfaction.

Useful indicators can be:
- Benefits achieved as outlined in the business case;
- Nature of the stakeholder correspondence (positive vs. negative);
- Number, nature and outcome of complaints and resolutions;
- Safety performance (e.g. lost time incidents, (near) fatal accidents; timely permissions/permits);
- Awards and formal appreciations received by stakeholders (e.g. recognition received in the media, publications and articles, awards received from relevant organisations);
- Number, nature and results of citizens' and other stakeholders' initiatives;
- Number, nature and results of lawsuits and other legal/contractual actions.

C.4. Project Results and Impact on the Environment

Excellent projects achieve outstanding results while keeping high performance levels. Such results are achieved as an outcome of excellent management and leadership. Their positive impact on the environment is also clearly visible.

Examples of project results could be:
- Products;
- Services;
- Changes (e.g. social, organisational, cultural);
- Financial benefits;
- Social impact;
- Market position;
- Intangible (e.g. knowledge);
- Intellectual property (e.g. technologies, systems, inventions).

C.4a. Realisation of results as defined in project objectives
Excellent projects realise the results as defined in the project objectives (A.2b.).

The definitions of objectives related to project results might be found in, for example:
- Project charter;
- Scope specification;
- Change project objectives;
- Organisation strategic plans;
- Technical specifications;
- Quality metrics;
- Acceptance criteria;
- Business case (e.g. for value to the sponsor, market share, profitability/ROI levels).

C.4b. Realisation of results beyond project objectives, including impact on environment
Excellent project management and leadership often lead to additional results beyond planned project objectives. These include positive impact on their environment (e.g. natural, organisational, business etc.).

Examples of results beyond objectives could be:
- Public recognition (e.g. media attention, or a structure that becomes a landmark);
- Sector recognition (e.g. becoming the benchmark);
- Awards;
- Repeat orders;
- New or improved methodologies, technologies and/or products i.e. innovation;
- Intellectual property rights;
- Knowledge and experience transfer;
- Implementation of lessons learnt in other activities;
- Long-term benefits (e.g. socio-economic);
- Long-term cost savings;
- Contribution to industry development.

Examples of positive impact on the natural environment could be:
- Outcome of waste reduction (e.g. materials, resources);
- Result of pollution levels (actual vs. planned);
- Outcome of use of raw vs. recycled material;
- Extent of use of renewable materials vs. non-renewables;
- Outcome of recycling management;
- Meeting ecological requirements/regulations;
- Certification according to health, safety and environmental standards (e.g. ISO 14000, OHSAS);
- Relation of planned/actual ecological indicators.

C.4c. Project performance

Excellent projects realise their results in an effective and efficient way and minimise their negative impact on the project environment.

The following indicators of results delivery effectiveness and efficiency should be considered:
- Cost level;
- On-time delivery;
- Usage of resources;
- Use of (renewable) materials and reduction of waste;
- Avoidance of negative environmental impact;
- Mitigation of negative social impact;
- Prevention of safety incidents;
- Cost of (non-) quality.

Annex A: Description of the Project Excellence Model

Annex B:
Scoring tables for the IPMA Project Excellence Model

Annex B: Scoring tables

Scoring table for People & Purpose and Processes & Resources areas

The following table should be used for scoring each sub-criterion within the People & Purpose and Processes & Resources areas.

PLAN Defining a sound approach	DO Applying an approach systematically	CHECK Monitoring and analysing results of the chosen approach	ACT Improving and integrating the approach	Score
An innovative approach is developed to meet the needs of the project	All relevant stakeholders are fully committed to the innovative/ significantly improved approach and systematically apply it	All relevant stakeholders are fully engaged in proactive forecasting of potential areas for improvement	All relevant stakeholders are fully engaged in the proactive improvement of the approach and integration beyond the project	up to 100
A proven approach is significantly improved to meet the needs of the project		Proactive forecasting of potential areas for improvement is driven by project leaders	Proactive improvement of the approach and integration within the project is driven by project leaders	up to 80
An adequate approach is clearly agreed by all relevant stakeholders and fully aligned with the needs of the project	The approach is systematically followed by all relevant stakeholders	Results of the approach are regularly monitored and analysed	Effective actions are taken whenever analysis shows potential for improvement	up to 60
An approach is agreed with some relevant stakeholders and partially aligned with the needs of the project	Key elements of the approach are followed by relevant key stakeholders	Significant variances from planned results are noticed by project leaders within a reasonable timeframe	All major variances observed in key areas of the project lead to improvement actions	up to 40
Some approach is agreed with some relevant stakeholders	Some elements of the approach are followed by some of the relevant stakeholders	Major variances in key areas are brought to the attention of project leaders	There are attempts to improve the approach when major variances occur	up to 20
No proof	No proof	No proof	No proof	0

Table 3: Scoring table for People & Purpose and Processes & Resources areas

Scoring table for Customer, Project Team and Other Stakeholder Satisfaction criteria

The following table should be used for scoring Customer, Project Team and Other Stakeholder Satisfaction criteria (C.1., C.2., C.3.).

Separate scoring should be conducted for each of these criteria. The lowest level sub-criteria (e.g. C.1a., C.1b.) are integrated within the scoring table (see first and second column below) and therefore should not be scored separately.

Perceived satisfaction level (C.1a./C.2a./C.3a.)	Expected satisfaction level according to indicators (C.1b./C.2b./C.3b.)	Link between the approach and satisfaction level (IPMA PEM areas A & B)	Comparison of the satisfaction level with the industry/sector benchmark	Score
Exceptional and expressed proactively	Fully supports exceptional satisfaction	The approach enabled the establishment of a new benchmark	A new benchmark established	up to 100
Exceptional		The approach directly led to exceptional satisfaction level	Outstanding in some areas	up to 80
Positive in all key areas	Positive in all key areas	Clear link in all key areas	Good in all key areas	up to 60
Positive in some areas	Positive in some areas	Clear link in some areas	Acceptable in most areas	up to 40
Neutral	Neutral	Weak link	Acceptable in some areas	up to 20
Negative	Negative	No proof, or approach clearly leads to dissatisfaction	No proof	0

Table 4: Scoring table for Customer, Project Team and Other Stakeholder Satisfaction criteria

Annex B: Scoring tables

Scoring table for Project Results criteria

The following table should be used for scoring the Project Results criteria (C.4.).

Sub-criteria C.4a. and C.4b. (Realisation of results as defined in project objectives and Realisation of results beyond project objectives) should be scored together, as both relate to various project results. Separate scoring should be conducted for sub-criterion C.4c. (Project performance).

Realisation of project objectives	Link between the approach and objectives realisation IPMA (PEM areas A & B)	Trends	Comparison of results with the industry/sector benchmark	Score
Substantially exceeded	The approach enabled the establishment of a new benchmark	Continuously above the benchmark	A new benchmark established	up to 100
Exceeded	The approach exceeded objectives	Continuously exceeding expectations	Outstanding in some areas	up to 80
All realised	Clear link in all key areas	Continuously positive in all key areas	Good in all key areas	up to 60
Majority realised	Clear link in some areas	Continuously positive in some areas	Acceptable in most areas	up to 40
Only partly realised	Weak link	Periodic	Acceptable in some areas	up to 20
No proof	No proof	No proof	No proof	0

Table 5: Scoring table for Project Results criteria

Annex C:
The IPMA Global Project Excellence Award assessment and its benefits

The IPMA Global Project Excellence Award assessment

IPMA annually awards project management prizes to project teams worldwide that achieve and can prove great feats in project management. The IPMA Project Excellence Model (IPMA PEM) is used as an assessment tool for projects that apply for the IPMA Global Project Excellence Awards.

IPMA has standardised processes for Small-/Medium-Sized projects (see the IPMA website) and Large- and Mega-Sized projects. The process for the Large- and Mega-Sized projects consists of the following steps:
- The IPMA Awards PMO and Awards Coordinator select trained IPMA award assessment teams and appoint team lead assessors (TLAs) for each application;
- The assessors carry out their first individual assessment;
- Each of the assessment teams discusses its findings and scores in a virtual team meeting and prepares a first judges report;
- The assessment team carries out a Site Visit and prepares a second judges report;
- The assessment team prepares a Feedback Report for the applicant organisation;
- In relevant applicant categories, the judges decide on:
  - Project finalists;
  - Bronze prize (bronze project excellence recognition);
  - Silver prize (silver project excellence recognition);
  - Gold prize (gold project excellence recognition).

The IPMA Global Project Excellence Award assessment process

1. **IPMA Award assessment teams and TLA assignment:** The IPMA Vice President, IPMA Awards Coordinator and the IPMA Awards PMO assign IPMA award assessors, the assessment teams and the TLAs. The appointed assessors for the current year must confirm their full commitment to participate in the full duration of the IPMA assessment process.
2. **First assessment result and first IPMA award judges meeting:** After receiving the application report, each IPMA award assessor carries out his/her individual assessment based on the IPMA PEM. The TLA consolidates and analyses the assessor results. During the virtual team meeting, the assessment team discusses the individual results with the objective of

reaching a common understanding. During this meeting, the assessors also compile a list of questions, topics for which additional information is needed and documents to be studied, to be provided at the Site Visit. The assessment team provides its results to the IPMA award judges in the first judges report. During their first meeting, the judges collect questions and topics for the assessment teams during the Site Visit and provides them to the TLAs.

3. **Site Visit and final IPMA award judges decision:** The TLA, with support from the IPMA awards PMO, organises the visit with the applicant. The purpose of the Site Visit is to collect additional information and perceptions for the final assessment of the project. During the Site Visit, the assessment team conducts interviews with all involved parties in the project. After the interviews. the TLA organises a team meeting to finalise the assessment results from the Site Visit as per the IPMA PEM assessment criteria. The consolidated final results from all assessment teams are provided to the award judges in a second judges report. During the second award judges meeting, the judges analyse the assessment result, checks additional questions with the TLAs and decide which projects qualify as finalist(s) and which are the projects receiving the bronze, silver and gold award. This decision is kept strictly confidential until the IPMA awards ceremony, at which the results are officially announced.

4. **Feedback Reports** are prepared by the assessment team and presented to each applicant by two judges after the awards ceremony.

The Site Visit

The Site Visit process starts with the preparation for the visit and focuses on the IPMA award assessment team interviews with all interested parties (stakeholders) of the applicant's project. The TLA is responsible for the consolidation of the assessment results and consensus of the team on these results.

Site Visit steps:
1. **Preparation for Site Visit:** The IPMA awards PMO provides the TLA with the rules for the Site Visit, such as travel rules, behaviour requirements during the Site Visit, etc. as agreed with the applicants, TLAs and Assessors. The agenda for the interviews with the interested parties is agreed between the assessment team and applicant. The assessors also prioritise the most important questions, topics and documents they want to talk about and see during the Site Visit to find further information necessary for the assessment.

2. **Site Visit and interviews:** The applicant presents the project and TLA presents the IPMA Global Project Excellence Award process and products. After these presentations, the interviews and document checks take place. During the interviews, the assessors seek proof for the IPMA PEM criteria and assess them.
3. **Feedback consolidation and consolidation on final assessment:** The assessment team consolidates the information from all interviews. The results from the Site Visit are consolidated and written up in a second judges report. The judges report consists of the findings of the assessment team as well as their recommendations to the judges. In parallel, the assessment team starts work on writing the Feedback Report for the applicant.

The award judges assessment

The judges play an important role during the assessment process. The judges receive initial information from each applicant and are in contact with the TLAs during the assessment process. Two award judges meetings are organised during the assessment.
1. During the first judges meeting (a virtual meeting), the award judges iterview the TLA and defines for each application which additional topics/ questions need to be covered during the site Visit. This information is provided to the respective TLAs.
2. During the second judges meeting (a physical meeting) every TLA presents the outcomes from the Site Visit. Based on this information and the consolidated results from the assessment (covering all IPMA PEM criteria) the award judges select the finalists and takes the final decision on the winners.

The award judges prepare feedback that is reviewed with the TLA and is integrated in the Feedback Report. The Feedback Report is a document that is created for each applicant individually by the assessment team. It provides the applicant with an overview of strengths and areas of improvement with respect to each criterion of the IPMA PEM.

The IPMA Global Project Excellence Award benefits

Benefits for stakeholders

A central component of the IPMA Global Project Excellence Award mission is to help organisations improve their performance in project management. Organisations can use the IPMA PEB not only to apply for the IPMA Global Project Excellence Award competition, but also as a management tool to achieve excellence in project management. The combined outcomes of the IPMA Global Project Excellence Award and experiences gathered by organisations are capitalised by educating business, government organisations, municipalities and communities on the benefits of improving their project management performance.

Organisations that reach the finalist level or become an award winner can reach a large audience and have the greatest chance for success in helping to spread the message about the benefits of following the project excellence concept and using the IPMA PEB to improve project performance.

Benefits for applicants

Organisations that reach the finalist level or become an award winner are recognised in front of a large international audience and join a select group of internationally acclaimed projects.

Applying for the award in itself gives a project team a ready-made opportunity to test their excellence in project management. If a project team uses the IPMA PEM to reflect on its own achievements, it will automatically identify improvements and actively address them.

The main benefit for applicants is in receiving feedback on the strengths and improvement potential of their project management. The project teams applying for the IPMA Global Project Excellence Award receive a detailed written Feedback Report from the IPMA assessment team of qualified and experienced global project experts in leading project management positions.

Benefits for finalists and winners

Finalists and winners of the IPMA Global Project Excellence Award will enjoy such benefits as:

- **The highest international honour for excellent project performance and worldwide recognition.** The IPMA Global Project Excellence Award is awarded to the project teams that achieve the best results based on the IPMA PEM, making them the most successful representatives of project management. The IPMA finalists and winners gain confidence and additional support from their stakeholders, which will enhance their further success. The project team members will also gain confidence in their capability to manage future projects, and this will enhance their career prospects.
- **Multi-dimensional marketing opportunities for the applicant's organisation on a worldwide scale.** The IPMA Global Project Excellence Award considerably enhances the prestige of IPMA award winners and finalists, because their names are officially published. The logo of the IPMA Global Project Excellence Award is available for company documents and publications. This enables the team to show that they are recognised as one of the most successful project teams. IPMA award winners and finalists are invited to pass on their experience of project excellence at the annual IPMA Project Management World Congress. This is an outstanding opportunity to show their status as a leading project management team and share experiences. The IPMA World Congress documents and other publications demonstrate the IPMA PEM and use the teams and organisations responsible as practical examples. Reaching the level of the IPMA Global Project Excellence Award is the result of long-term dedication to excellence and improvement in project management.
- **Award continuity:** The IPMA Global Project Excellence Award is given once a year to a project of a given organisation but the same company/organisation can participate in the following year and demonstrate how it has applied the improvements suggested by the IPMA award assessment team.

References

1. International Project Management Association (2015), IPMA Individual Competence Baseline (IPMA ICB®), Version 4.0

2. International Project Management Association (2013), IPMA Organisational Competence Baseline (IPMA OCB®), Version 1.0

3. European Foundation for Quality Management (2012), EFQM Excellence Model 2013

4. ISO TC/258 Project, programme and portfolio management (2012), ISO 21500:2012 Guidance on project management, Edition 1

5. United Nations Global Compact (2004), The Ten Principles of UN Global Compact, https://www.unglobalcompact.org/what-is-gc/mission/principles

6. United Nations Global Compact, Accenture Management Consulting (2013), UN Global Compact—Accenture CEO Study on Sustainability 2013, https://www.accenture.com/sk-en/insight-un-global-compact-ceo-study-sustainability-2013

7. International Project Management Association (2015), IPMA Code of Ethics and Professional Conduct

Made in the USA
Monee, IL
10 October 2025

31809303R00072